NEW READINGS OF SPIRITUAL NARRATIVE FROM THE FIFTEENTH TO THE TWENTIETH CENTURY

Secular Force and Self-Disclosure

NEW READINGS OF SPIRITUAL NARRATIVE FROM THE FIFTEENTH TO THE TWENTIETH CENTURY

Secular Force and Self-Disclosure

Edited by

Phebe Davidson

Studies in Religion and Society
Volume 31

The Edwin Mellen Press
Lewiston/Queenston/Lampeter

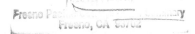

Library of Congress Cataloging-in-Publication Data

New readings of spiritual narrative from the fifteenth to the
  twentieth century : secular force and self-disclosure / edited by
  Phebe Davidson.
      p.   cm. -- (Studies in religion and society ; v. 31)
  Includes bibliographical references.
  ISBN 0-7734-8878-2
  1. Religious biography--History and criticism.   I. Davidson,
  Phebe.   II. Series: Studies in religion and society ; v. 31.
  BL71.5.N48   1995
  270'.092'2--dc20   95-6141
                                                                       CIP

This is volume 31 in the continuing series
Studies in Religion and Society
Volume 31 ISBN 0-7734-8878-2
SRS Series ISBN 0-88946-863-X

A CIP catalog record for this book is available from the British Library.

The Edwin Mellen Press   The Edwin Mellen Press
       Box 450   Box 67
  Lewiston, New York   Queenston, Ontario
   USA 14092-0450   CANADA L0S 1L0

The Edwin Mellen Press, Ltd.
Lampeter, Dyfed, Wales
UNITED KINGDOM SA48 7DY

Printed in the United States of America

CONTENTS

i   Editor's Preface

1   *Catherine Jones West*
Re-envisioning Woman's Place: The Body Politic and Spiritual in
L'Avision- Christine.

13   *Phebe Davidson*
Margery Kempe and the Main Stream

37   *Joseph Zornado*
Paul's Epistles and John Bunyan's *Grace Abounding to the Chief of
Sinners*

51   *Karen S. Nulton*
Creating and Containing: Scriptural Uses in Two Early American
Captivity Narratives

69   *Joanne M. Gaudio*
"Praying for an Earthquake": Personal Narrative as Colonial Conversion
in "The Autobiography of Increase Mather"

93   *Manuela Mourăo*
Intertextuality and Feminist Intervention in *New Portuguese Letters*

Preface

Spiritual narrative, generally recognized in the world of letters in western civilization as that narrative genre which describes an individual's journey to and relationship with God, has a lengthy and at times curiously submerged history. This submergence, it would seem, has gone hand in hand with an increasing secularization of vision on the part of society at large, so that narratives perceived as relatively secular, like the early American narratives of Indian captivity, may have embedded in them the rhetorical and narrative strategies of spiritual narrative. These rhetorical and narrative strategies may go largely unrecognized on a conscious level, although they may, at the same time, resonate within the reader's consciousness in a variety of ways. Conversely, religious or spiritual narratives, like Margery Kempe's account of her religious vocation, may have embedded in them twin narratives of secular journeys that can go similarly unrecognized, and that also resonate in a number of interesting and frequently startling ways. Not surprisingly, the audience for each narrative of self-disclosure, be it religious or secular, has often tended to read the narrative it had come looking for, when in fact other narratives were present in the text as well.

This volume offers an eclectic assortment of new readings of spiritual narrative, indicative of both the liveliness and the breadth of current scholarly interest in spiritual narrative as a subject for serious intellectual discussion and exploration. What all of these essays have in common, aside from the rather broad subject designation of spiritual narrative, is a recognition that spiritual narrative has almost always co-existed with its secular counterpart, often in the same text, and that it has served (and continues to serve) as the paradigm for narrative forms heretofore viewed in other contexts, whether as fiction, autobiography, or political tract. The complexity of vision offered in these readings is compelling and provocative.

Catherine Jones West, for instance, finds in Christine de Pizan's *L'Avision--Christine* "a complex, hybrid work" that is not solely a spiritual narrative, but a political analysis and critique as well, one that serves to envision woman's place in the world in startling new ways while my own exploration of *The Boke of Margery Kempe* suggests that Kempe's religious autobiography embodies, along with the experience of a fifteenth-century English Catholic mystic, the narrative of a woman's emergence into a distinctly useful *secular* realm of empowerment and freedom of behavior. Joseph Zornado, in discussing pre-textual occasions for John Bunyan's seventeenth-century *Grace Abounding to the Chief of Sinners*, introduces both insight and grounds for debate about the textual antecedents in scripture and in ecclesiastical autobiography of much subsequent English autobiography. Karen Nulton and Joanne Gaudio, both dealing with colonial American narratives, find respectively that spiritual narrative was a means for women to define themselves in the generally proscribed position of narrators of war, and for at least one man to employ the personal spiritual autobiography as a type for national, historical narrative. Manuela Mourão, in discussing the 1971 *New Portuguese Letters*, confronts the heavily intertextual feminist agenda of twentieth-century women who are political activists facing a "fierce patriarchal, Catholic society."

Certainly, this volume makes no claim to be exhaustive or definitive. The texts and writers under discussion, from the fifteenth-century *L'Avision Christine* and its author, Christine de Pizan, through the twentieth-century *New Portuguese Letters* by Maria Isabel Barreno, Maria Velho da Costa, and Maria Teresa Horta, are arranged chronologically, although the intertextual nature of the discussions (which includes such apparently disparate texts as St. Paul's epistles, Dante's *La Divina Commedia* and the seventeenth-century epistolary fiction, *Letters of a Portuguese Nun*) makes chronology a problematic arrangement. Like chronology, the nature of spiritual narrative itself becomes problematic as the writers contributing to this volume explore the personal, political, economic, and literary ramifications of the works under discussion as well as their spiritual significance.

If *New Readings of Spiritual Narrative* is anything, it is a collection of work intended to provoke further thought and discussion. To borrow the words of Lillian S. Robinson, in her foreword to *Revealing Lives* (ed. Susan Groag Bell and Marilyn Yalom. Albany: State University of New York Press, 1990), these essays ". . .do more than simply preach to those already convinced of the centrality of large social categories for the analysis of individual lives. . ." (vii)-- they discover within their subject new complexities and new directions for thought.

Phebe Davidson

Re-envisioning Woman's Place: The Body Politic and Spiritual in *L'Avision--Christine*

Catherine Jones West

Converse College

Written on the heels of the debate concerning misogynistic elements in *The Romance of the Rose*, Christine de Pizan's *L'Avision--Christine* redresses the harm done to women by portraying female characters of great dignity and by rethinking specific trends in Western thought that have stressed the derivative, immoral nature of women. Intended as both a vision and warning, as the play on the verb *aviser* in the title suggests, this text criticizes the reign of Charles VI and suggests the advisability of heeding the reforms proposed by Philip of Burgundy. A complex, hybrid work, *L'Avision--Christine* portrays the disorder that haunted the political and intellectual life of fifteenth-century France, and relates that chaos to the disarray Christine felt upon losing her father, her husband, and her patron.

Attempting to come to terms with the "anomalous" role these deaths forced her to play, she couches her criticism of France's monarch and of society's treatment of women in a wealth of Biblical references, and in echoes of Boethius's *Consolation of Philosophy* and of Dante's *La Divina Commedia*. Autobiography and history merge as she evokes her varied experiences as daughter, wife, mother, and writer; relating her life as a widow, deprived of the support of a husband or patron, to that of France under the ineffective leadership of Charles VI.

Endorsing a less conservative view of women's place than found in some of her earlier works, she follows the study of her homeland's history with the story of her own itinerary. She thus furthers what Cynthia Ho identifies as one of the objectives of *The Book of the City of Ladies:*

> In addition to presenting history for the first time from the woman's viewpoint, our narrator has another agenda: to complement this universal history with the story of an individual, also from the female perspective. (2)

L'Avision--Christine opens with the words:

> One evening, halfway through my pilgrimage, I found myself tired from the long journey and longing for a place to rest. (1)

The sentence brings to mind Dante's "nel mezzo del cammin di nostra vita," though Christine uses the first person singular, rather than the plural, emphasizing the personal nature of her "autobiographical manifesto," as Sylvia Huot refers to this work. *L'Avision*, like *La Divina Commedia,* consists of three parts whose progression is one of linear ascent, but the work's movement is also centripetal, moving from the historical to the personal, from the abstract to the particular.

It has been said that the three parts of *L'Avision* coincide with the three phases of Christine's life. In her introduction to her 1932 edition, Sister Mary Louise Towner observes:

> May we not see in the three universes, the material the intellectual, and that of divine things, depicted in *L'Avision*, an analogy to the three stages in the life of Christine? Disheartened with the tragic events in her early life, she sought solace among her books. The day came when the din of civil strife drowned the voice of learning, then Christine sought refuge and comfort beyond the intellectual life in the peace and quiet of a spiritual life within the cloister. (46)

Sylvia Huot agrees that *L'Avision* portrays Christine's life as a flight form the changeable, material world, "as a movement from biological to literary love and fruition, a movement characterized by the transcendence of the physical and sensible" (368). Similarly, Maureen Slatterly Durley sees in Christine's interlocutors three distinct ideals, personified as mothers, who appear "in an ascending scale of realist order in which the life the spirit is superior to the material life of the flesh" (30).

Though the work culminates with the lessons of Dame Philosophy, who is also addressed as Dame Theology, the emphasis seems less on an ascetic renunciation of the world than on the need for Christine to cease lamenting the losses that enabled her to devote herself to writing. Just when the heroine accedes to the highest realms of knowledge, she is enjoined to celebrate the events that prompted her to develop her understanding and play an active role in the worlds of literature and politics. The movement of the work therefore reinscribes the figure of the mother in the life of the state, denying that literary and biological fruition are mutually exclusive roles--one being the domain of men, the other of women. She therefore reappropriates metaphors of birthing and creativity found in texts by male writers, and claims for women greater spheres of influence.

This process of reappropriation is evident in the opening page of the vision, which evokes Christine's journey, in sleep, to a tenebrous region where she beholds the creation of human beings from Chaos. As is typical in her writings, Christine uses familiar intertexts, but adapts them to her main themes. Her first vision is that of a man of inestimable size who is shadowed by woman of even greater proportions. Whereas the male figure, Chaos, appears as a passive figure who merely consumes that which Dame Nature provides, the female figure is constantly active, carefully shaping the forms of those who will people the world. Dame Nature is referred to as a "wise provider" who has no visible or palpable body. Chaos, however, appears as a very physical being whose stomach and mouth have "encompassed the ends of the earth," and whose appetite is insatiable. By stressing that Dame Nature contributes the form of human life while Chaos merely serves as the body in which her creations mature,

Christine rejects Aristotle's contention that the male is the source of the form or essence of the embryo, while the female provides only the nutrition necessary to sustain it.

In addition, the narrator refrains from emphasizing, in the style of Jean de Meun, the seduction of the female body, choosing instead to emphasize other aspects of procreation. Celebrating the generative potential of women, she also suggests the role they should play in the education of children. Once Christine's body has been formed, it is Nature's handmaiden who sees to Christine's education:

> The wise woman brought me what my body needed for nourishment, thereby causing it to grow still more. She also developed my understanding, allowing me to comprehend the varying configurations of the entrails of the figure. (5)

Distinguishing between the description of generation in *L'Avision* and *The Romance of the Rose*, Sylvia Huot writes:

> In Jean de Meun's treatment, the central metaphor of generation informs a poetic of desire, a quest for possession and consummation. Christine's feminized version subordinates the role of desire and informs a movement leading not to possession but to production. (367)

Having completed the first stage of her education and then traveled to a land of great renown, Christine meets Libera, a crowned princess who has borne and nurtured all of France's monarchs. Unlike Dame Nature, she has a physical body; a body that has been abused by the children reared on her milk. Whereas Chaos's stomach extends so far that Christine does not feel she could explore all of its recesses in one lifetime, Libera's sides have been completely trampled:

> Turning my gaze in that direction, I saw her white tender sides, blackened by blows and crushed as far as her intestines. (25)

A symbol of the ravages suffered by France under corrupt rulers and a reminder of the physical and intellectual harm endured by women, the crowned princess figures as an image of Christine in her more fragile moments. In Part III of *L'Avision*, when the heroine laments the death of the men who provided for her emotional and financial support, she echoes the phrases of her first interlocutor. Though Sister Mary Louise Towner suggests that Christine chose the name Libera because it signifies, as does *FRANCS*, freedom, she may also have been thinking of the Libera of ancient Rome. A goddess of rebirth and renewal that Christine would have known through the writings of Ovid and Augustine, Libera was first celebrated in a cult with Ceres and Liber, but was later forgotten as the cult of her male counterpart became increasingly popular. By refiguring the goddess Libera as a mortal woman who undergoes great suffering, and by suggesting the omnipresence of the figure named Chaos, Christine is setting the tone for the ensuing critique of those who think the world is theirs to plunder. Longing to encourage in her people a less rapacious attitude toward their homeland, Libera befriends Christine and asks that she be her scribe.

Libera begins her narration by tracing the origin of the Franks back to Troy, following the tradition of French historians, but perhaps also lending her text a sense of foreboding by beginning with a historical referent that we associate with war. Christine continues the work of *The Book of the City of Ladies* by revising how history has portrayed certain women. When she evokes Helen of Troy, she avoids making of her an Eve or Pandora figure, responsible for the city's downfall, and instead stresses the brilliant civilization that she helped found. She also emphasizes the harm that has befallen those who have injured women:

> Several kingdoms have been destroyed, as I can not doubt when I consider the example of Jacob's daughter, Dinah. She was ravished by the king of Sichem. Amon pretended to be sick in order to have Tamar, his sister, and for this he was killed by his brother Absalon. The abduction of Helen by Paris resulted in the destruction of Troy. The historians tell that a king of France was sent into exile for this reason. Tarquin the Proud inspired Lucretia, the chaste lady of Rome, to kill herself, and for this, he and his son were exiled. (45-46)

Libera's story dwells on the harm her country has suffered at the hand of aggressive rulers, emphasizing the darker moments of France's history. Her words will find an echo in the final part of the vision, when the primary narrator --Christine herself--recounts her own experiences. Deeply troubled by the mutations her personal life, as well as the life of her adopted homeland, had recently undergone, Christine's vision becomes a meditation on the role of misfortune in human existence, and a plea for a new ethic that ceases to promote "male" values. She describes the varied rulers of France as either good or bad gardeners, suggesting that we should see ourselves as stewards, rather than as masters, of nature.

Though Libera occasionally longs for a Samson figure who will solve the problems of the body politic, she also indicates that her female interlocutor might best affect the behavior of the people. Selecting the young heroine of *L'Avision* to be her scribe, she tacitly agrees with the Christine of *The Book of the City of Ladies* who said that women, if they turned to writing, would refrain from perpetuating male myths. Having suffered repeatedly at the hands of her children, Libera hopes that her scribe's words will encourage a gentler behavior: "They (my children) might be like loyal and true children who still need the milk of the loving mother, but who spare her breast by not nursing so hard it bleeds" (52-53). Enjoined by Libera to educate the future leaders of France, Christine finds herself reinscribed in the life of the body politic. She therefore strikes off in search of the ideal that might best inform the works she is to address to her friend's children.

In Part II, *L'Avision* moves from a consideration of history to a consideration of the life of the mind, dwelling, in particular, on dominant trends in Greek thought. Christine writes that she arrives at a place called the second Athens, where she sees another female figure who appears as a multi-colored shade and who hovers above those engaged in various intellectual debates. A reminder of the years when Christine devoted herself to learning, this section, as Durley suggests, introduces an image of the mother that lies between Libera's suffering, earthly body and Dame Philosophy's bodiless serenity, as evoked in the final part of the text. There, however, where Christine expects to find a refuge from the chaos encountered during the first part of her dream vision, she finds still more disarray, the clerics of the university engaged in numerous discussions. Dame Opinion explains that she and her daughters were formed at the same time as Adam, and thereby denies the tradition that holds Eve responsible for the fall of man from a state of innocence which admitted neither truth nor falsehood, good nor evil. Instead of upholding that Eve alone was blameworthy, Adam being only the victim of her disrespect, Dame Opinion insists that she was formed simultaneously with Adam:

> Know that I was formed along with Adam. I am the daughter of Ignorance, and desire for knowledge engendered me. The first man and woman bit into the apple because of my deceitful order. (61)

Having learned that human understanding is haunted by ignorance and characterized by incertitude, Christine asks Opinion to help her reconsider the content of her works. As she foregrounds her activity as a writer, Christine avoids suggesting that the inspiration for her works comes from a divine, immutable source, and instead depicts the subject as process, engaged in a dialectic of visions and revisions.

Better understanding the life of the state and that of the mind, and anxious to find a world less chaotic than they, Christine continues her journey through the university to see what might be learned at its highest levels. The description of the moment when she first beholds Dame Philosophy recalls Dante's description of his arrival in paradise, with certain secular variations. Where he sees nine rows of angels, she sees the nine liberal arts appearing as women, a priestly caste suggesting the role women play as teachers of culture. Christine engages in a conversation with Dame Philosophy who identifies herself as the woman who appeared to Boetius in his prison cell. Echoing the arguments expressed in the *Consolation of Philosophy,* Christine then has her interlocutor voice arguments whose slant becomes gradually more feminist. Dame Philosophy first encourages Christine to feel gratitude for her parents and children, and to remember that ill-fortune favors us when it demonstrates the illusory nature of traditional comforts. In a phrase that rings less true to her source, Philosophy concludes that Christine should cease lamenting the loss of her husband and instead recognize that his death allowed her to develop her person in ways that defied society's expectations for women.

If Christine's warning/vision concludes with the lessons of Dame Philosophy, a woman who, unlike Libera and Dame Opinion, has transcended the incertitude of earthly existence, it is not only to indicate Christine's spiritual progress; it is also because this allegorical figure brings the knowledge that best enables the heroine to accept the role she was obliged to play after the death of her husband. Emphasizing the cyclical, as well as the linear, movement of this work, Christine Reno writes:

> The third part of *L'Avision*, at the same time that it brings one of Christine's journeys to a close, leaves her on the threshold of another one. (. . . .) To adapt an image from Plato, Christine is in the position of the philosopher of *The Republic*, who, having ascended to a vision of the Good, must now redescend on a mission of salvation into the cave of society from which he came. (152)

Having acknowledged the difficulty of fulfilling accepted gender roles while leading an active intellectual life, Christine thanks Dame Philosophy for the encouragement she has brought and addresses her as God: "I thank you, who are God, who is you, in such a way I cannot explain" (159). Throughout the first and third parts of her vision, Christine evokes a God who appears as a stern patriarch seeking signs of weakness in his children; an attempt, perhaps, to inspire greater sobriety in those whose comportment was resulting in civil war. In the conversation with Dame Philosophy/Theology and in the distance separating her form the punitive patriarch evoked in other sections of the text, we can also see the author's attempt to view her own anomalous activity as a woman writer in fifteenth-century France and the life of the spirit in less traditionally gendered terms.

Envisioning an intellectual discourse that would be dialogic, rather than animated by a longing for possession and mastery, Christine casts herself in the roles of both narrator and interlocutor. Seeking to make sense of the disarray that had come to haunt her life, she uses the form of the dream vision, not so much to convey religious truth, but rather to suggest the need for political reform and to represent the varied forms women's creative potential can assume both within and beyond the familiar world of the home.

BIBLIOGRAPHY

Works by Christine de Pizan:

Christine de Pizan. *A Medieval Woman's Mirror of Honor: The Treasure of the City of Ladies.* Trans. Charity Cannon Willard. New York: Persea Books, 1989.

_____. *Christine's L'Avision: A Translation and Commentary.* Trans. Catherine Jones West. Studies in Medieval and Renaissance Texts: Pegasus, forthcoming.

_____. *L'Avision--Christine.* Ed. Sister Mary Louise Towner. The Catholic University of America. Studies in Roman Languages and Literatures. Vol. VI, 1922. New York: AMS Press, 1969.

_____. *La Querelle de la Rose: Letters and Documents.* Ed. Joseph L. Baird and John R. Kane. Chapel Hill: University of North Carolina Press, 1978.

Works About Christine de Pizan

Bornstein, Diane, ed. *Ideals for Women in the Works of Christine de Pizan.* Michigan Consortium for Medieval and Early Modern Studies, 1981.

Brown-Grant, Rosalind. "*L'Avision--Christine:* Autobiographical Narrative or Mirror for the Prince?" *Politics, Gender, and Genre: The Political Thought of Christine de Pizan.* Ed. Margaret Brabant. Boulder: Westview Pres, 1992, 95-112.

Ho, Cynthia. "Communal and Individual Autobiography in Christine de Pizan's *Book of the City of Ladies.*" CEA CRITIC, Special Edition: *Re-evaluating the Boundaries of Autobiography: Theory, Practice and Pedagogy.* Forthcoming.

Huot, Sylvia. "Seduction and Sublimation: Christine de Pizan, Jean de Meun, and Dante." *Romance Notes* 24, 3 (Spring 1985): 361-373.

_____. "Christine de Pizan: Feminism and Irony.:" *Seconda Miscellanea di Studi e Ricerche sul Quattrocento Francese*. Ed. Franco Simone, Jonathan Beck, and Gianni Mombello. Chambery/Torino: Centre d'Etudes Franco-Italien, 1981, 1299-132.

_____. "The Preface to the *Avision--Christine* in ex-Phillips 128." *Reinterpreting Christine*. Ed. earl Jeffrey Richards, with Joan Williamson, Nadia Margolis, and Christine Reno. Athens: University of Georgia Press, 1992. 207-227.

Richards, Earl Jeffrey. "Christine de Pizan and the Question of Feminist Rhetoric." *Teaching Language through Literature* 22.2 (April 1983): 15-24.

Willard, Charity Cannon. *Christine de Pizan: Her Life and Works*. New York: Persea, 1984.

_____. "Women and Marriage Around 1400: Three Views." *Fifteenth Century Studies* 17 (1990): 475-484.

Margery Kempe and the Main Stream

Phebe Davidson

University of South Carolina at Aiken

That women in western culture have long occupied the margin of a cultural complex that privileges the masculine has become a standard commonplace among feminist critics. The relationship of the margin to the mainstream, however, remains problematic--at least insofar as one cannot exist without the other. In other words, each serves to define the other and thus, in some rather intriguing ways, is not only necessary to its existence, but part of that existence. Thus, a woman--a marginal figure in, say, fifteenth-century manuscript culture--is in some sense a part of the mainstream that denies her voice. She subscribes to the culture and, either by accepting her marginalism or by subverting and circumventing it, participates in that culture and causes it to flourish. At the same time, the mainstream forces that would silence her capitulate, defining her voice as a silence but not, in fact, silencing it effectively, so that the woman's metaphorical voice becomes part of the background blanket of cultural white noise.

I have argued elsewhere that if the idea of a tradition presupposes that each generation of writers knows the work of its predecessors (as for instance, Henry James knew Augustine's *Confessions*), then in one sense there was no appropriate literary tradition for the early woman writer of autobiography. The genre, which had been dominated since its inception by men, supplied no appropriate public mode for women. Such women's autobiographical texts as were published were seen more as oddities than as legitimate inscriptions in an unfolding tradition. Yet, inarguably, they were published and served as part of the cultural fabric of their own time. The inception and execution of such texts was fraught with complexity. Frequently, the larger society created in the woman who desired to narrate her life an autobiographer who, if she could read, did not have access to the texts of other women, or who, denied literacy, would have been unable to read the texts had they been available to her. In other instances, a woman's writing (inscribed in common vernacular rather than in Latin) was simply not defined as a literate text.

The result, at least in western civilization, was a sort of discontinuous tradition based on women's common experience of life in particular cultural and political settings--an experience encoded in their first person narratives. If, as I would suggest, the central element in all these texts is woman's response to cultural and political structures, and if in western culture that tradition remained (at least until the mid-nineteenth century) largely discontinuous, then there is a dual critical problem in discussing the autobiographies of women; the task of identifying the shared responses encoded in the texts is unavoidably yoked to the difficulty of placing the texts themselves in a tradition that might be argued not to exist at all. A way to resolve these two aspects of the problem is offered by *The Book of Margery Kempe.* This volume is the dictated autobiography of a fifteenth-century English mystic, who makes it abundantly clear that she has no desire for the life of a nun, yet who insists upon the validity of her unorthodox religious vocation, thereby creating a problem fully as intriguing textually as socially.

For those interested in autobiographical texts in English, Kempe's text marks a beginning. It is the earliest written autobiographical narrative in vernacular English language. It is the sort of literary artifact that can reasonably be expected to have relevance to later autobiographical work by women, both in form and in the themes it touches. Kempe began her *Book* in 1436, as a spiritual autobiography, and indeed it is profoundly concerned with matters of the author's religious growth. Importantly, however, it is also nearly obsessed with the nature of language and the uses to which that language can be put. In a narrative that traces the author's progress from her initial conversation with Christ through the formidable and obdurate obstacles of convincing her husband that they should live chastely, and of securing ecclesiastical endorsement for her religious calling, *The Book of Margery Kempe* details the author's conversion and call to live as a wife of Christ **in the world**. This worldliness--and Kempe's unflagging insistence upon it--are unprecedented in English letters. Both the life and the text, in a more auspicious intellectual and social climate, might have done much to shatter the received views of woman's role in flesh and spirit alike. Yet Kempe's highly public career argues that she was not as thoroughly marginalized as may first appear, even though the text demonstrates an the difficulty of its (and its writer's) path. The text specifically identifies Kempe's peculiar gift of uncontrolled and uncontrollable weeping (also variously described as roaring or crying) for the Passion of Christ, a gift of the spirit manifested in the flesh that often caused Kempe to be reviled. Yet the text insists absolutely on the author's right to employ the word, both spoken and written, despite the conventions of discourse and society that might have kept her silent in much the same way that it insists on the righteous necessity of her fits of weeping.

In part because of the lengthy disappearance (several hundred years) of Kempe's manuscript, English autobiography developed without her, evolving for the most part in a succession of male-authored texts whose writers were familiar with the work of their literary predecessors. Not surprisingly, there emerged certain literary and generic conventions. The connection of reader and writer and reader-as-writer/writer-as-reader guaranteed as much. Yet, as Kempe's book apparently demonstrates, a comparable continuous literary tradition simply did not exist in the autobiographical writing (or in Kempe's case, composing and dictation) of women, many of whom were illiterate (or so scholarship used to tell us with fair regularity) and whose work (if it were somehow written) was more likely to remain unpublished, whose position in society dictated different concerns and a different audience from those of male writers. Yet there was a tradition in the lives of saints, particularly female saints, developing on the continent and widely disseminated orally even in the northern reaches of England, so that for Kempe and others like her, there was at least some cultural basis for identification, even if conventional literacy was not available.

It is important here to recognize a separation between audience and writer, audience and editor. A woman writer was apt to find herself in the position of writing "for women" in the sense that she was writing out of the "woman's sphere" about women's concerns, but the editorial presence she needed to satisfy was, at this date, exclusively male--often personified in the person of a masculine amanuensis. Women also found, it would seem, a vernacular culture that set them a venue in which their stories could be related, and (if desired) modeled upon other stories heard or read. Still, without the sanction of men, the "literary" woman could not hope that her work would ever be known beyond a small, relatively intimate circle. Such, at least in part, was the case of the Kempe text. And because the Kempe text disappeared from general sight soon after its inscription, it retains a kind of purity. Denied its place in the developing tradition, it stands as a model of female autobiography that neither influenced nor contaminated succeeding texts, but that nevertheless underscores the marked similarities of women's life stories as they evolve from the spiritual tradition in English.[1]

What is known of Margery Burnham Kempe's life is not hard to recount

---

[1]Karma Lochrie expresses deep concern that the Kempe text can be "made to serve modern generic expectation at the expense of its mystical content. . ."(61), and while this a valid and conscientious worry, there remains some use in reading the text not solely as a mystical document. It's author, after all, embraced at least some elements of a secular experience combined with the enactment *in the world* of a religious vocation.

and serves to underscore a number of ways in which Kempe existed outside the "mainstream" of European life. The town where she was born and grew to adulthood was, to be sure, a busy port, but it existed on the northern edge of European commerce; she was the daughter of a locally prominent man, but not a member of the nobility; as a daughter, wife, and mother, she exercised her influence outside of the main areas of government and religion controlled by men; she was called to a religious vocation that cast her outside the kinds of religious vocations recognized in her town or her country; as a religious pilgrim, she was ridiculed and to some extent ostracized by her fellows. Yet she was simultaneously a part of a main stream of life developing at the time; as a religious mystic she moved in the company of saints whose stories were well known; as a bride of Christ she wrung acceptance of her vocation from a frequently hostile church, something she could hardly have done without some mainstream tolerance for her claim; as a travelling religious, she accrued an enthusiastic popular following, becoming a celebrity of considerable fame. This achievement alone, I would suggest, identifies her in some way with the "mainstream" of popular life in England at the time, as does the central nature of her family's position in the town where she grew up.

Margery Kempe was born in Bishop's Lynn, the daughter of John Burnham (or Brunham, as it is spelled in the Guild records of Lynn). Her father was a prosperous citizen who served Lynn as mayor five times. In 1394, John Kempe, her husband, became one of the four chamberlains of Lynn. On October 16, 1413, John Burnham died (Meech, xlviii-xlix). For other events in Kempe's life, we are dependent upon her text, verified insofar as that was possible by Sanford Brown and Hope Emily Allen. Thus, we know that she was probably born in 1373 and that in 1393, at the age of 20, she married John Kempe, who was prosperous enough though not so prominent as her father.

The following year she delivered her first child and commenced her lifelong dalliance with Christ, to whom she was called in a mystical marriage that she would dramatize while living as a free and uncloistered woman. In 1413, on

June 23, she and her husband privately agreed to live chaste, making their formal vow of mutual chastity before the Bishop of Lincoln later that summer. Probably subsequent to her father's death in October of that year, she went on pilgrimage to the Holy Land and Italy. The precise chronological connection between her father's death and the pilgrimage is uncertain; however, Clarissa Atkinson's belief that the death of her father may have been financially and psychologically enabling for Kempe seems to be in keeping with her character.

On November 9, 1414, in Rome, she celebrated her marriage to the Godhead, and subsequently wore only white. She returned to England in 1415, and in 1417 made a briefer pilgrimage to Spain. On her return to England she was imprisoned at Leicester, tried for heresy, and finally acquitted. About 1418 she returned to Lynn, where her husband (now an invalid) and a son who was visiting from Germany both died sometime in 1431. In 1433 she resumed her travels, visiting Norway, Danzig, and Aachen. Sometime in 1436 the priest who served as her second and final amanuensis[2] began work on revising Book I and writing down of Book II of Kempe's book.

Like many women before and since, Margery Burnham Kempe was caught between the equally compelling needs to speak and to remain silent. Her text begins with the author in childbed, facing the confessor to whom she needs to reveal some dark and private sin. This secret sin and its burden of damnation standing on one side, and the sharply reproving confessor to whom she could not bring herself to speak on the other, it is small wonder that she relates of herself (in typically garrulous and oblique fashion) "this creature went out of her mind and was wondrously vexed and labored with spirits for half a year, eight weeks, and odd days" (*BMK* 1).

---

[2]The first scribe to work on transcribing the book died, leaving behind a manuscript that was illegible to his successor until such time as God made him able to read it. Consequently, some time elapsed during which Kempe was able to amend the manuscript being read to her by the second amanuensis, before the text was concluded.

The reader must remember that both Margery Kempe and the confessor introduced on the first page of her narrative were products of their time, constructs of the very specific fifteenth-century audience for whom Kempe was later to devise her book. That audience would almost certainly have been familiar with theological dispute concerning the validity of a confession made to a tainted confessor, and the implications that in such an exchange the penitent's soul might be imperilled. Thus, it is likely that Kempe and her audience alike were capable of exerting rather vigorous disputational (and political) pressure on the church itself. The preeminent position in Kempe's text of this confrontation between a woman and her priest suggests that there is, for the writer (and by extension for some portion of her audience), tremendous importance in her refusal to speak to *this* particular priest, in her determination to *select* her own audience.

The confessor had on his side the weight of the Church, the absolute priestly power to judge and to bestow or withhold absolution. Margery Kempe occupied the considerably less powerful position of a woman in a male-dominated society. Additionally, she had just been through a long and difficult birth and feared for her life.

The patriarchal religious discourse that created this pair, a "ghostly confessor" who was the practical representative of patriarchy and the woman not yet recovered from childbirth who was the unclean figure at his mercy, and who required the purification of confession and absolution, articulated a network of tensions that have persisted into the present, tensions that require particular strategies of the female writer who, although marginalized, is arguably as central to the culture that would silence her. The woman has a need to make herself heard in difficult circumstances and, not surprisingly, arrogatates spiritual authority to validate her narrative of self-disclosure.

As a woman, Margery Kempe was barred from preaching, although she insisted on her right to speak of God without preaching. We can be fairly sure that Kempe profited by the example of Julian of Norwich (from whom Kempe would seek validation of her calling in 1413), whose question, "But because I am a woman, ought I therefore to believe that I should not tell you of the goodness of God, when I saw . . . his will that it be known?" (*Showings*, 135) bears such close relevance to Kempe's lifelong efforts to be heard. We can be equally sure, however, that Kempe was also profiting from other examples that would encourage her belief that she belonged in the world--an alternative that would require unusual circumstances and exceptional determination if it were to work out.

An alternative mode of religious expression, which found Kempe (or, as I am tempted to believe, was found by her) was weeping, a spontaneous outburst of crying prompted by her pity and horror at the passion of Christ. In describing this ungentle gift, Kempe tells her reader,

> . . . with the crying, [she] wrested her body, turning from one side to the other and waxed all blue and livid, like the color of lead. Then folk spat at her for horror of the sickness. (*BMK* 92)

In spite of the Church's acknowledgment of the legitimacy of similar manifestations of grace by female mystics on the European continent, Kempe's own gift was not readily accepted in England. One friar even barred her from church attendance when he was preaching rather than endure the disruption her fits of weeping always entailed. In this way, he denied her access to the Word, and to the sermon of the day, a form of discourse which she loved, although denied the right to employ it. To this exclusion, and to the perhaps deeper exclusion of women from dominant discourse for which it stands as emblem, Margery Kempe, mystic and woman in the world, responded in two ways. One was the persistent eruption of her alternate language of crying, weeping, and finally roaring for the Lord; the other was the creation, after a substantial and public career, of the manuscript we know as her book. Combining as it does "the factual and the spiritual" (Bottrall 2), *The Book of Margery Kempe* employs the language of the day simultaneously to affirm the truth of its writer's religious vocation, which involves substantially different expression than conventional discourse, and to challenge conventional expectations of womanly behavior.

The central problem for Margery Kempe, at the outset of her narrative, was to find a way to align her own innermost and highly subjective understanding of her situation with an arrangement or presentation of that situation that might prove acceptable to the world at large, a world whose sensibilities had been defined by a particular set of social and religious convictions. The audience supplied by the world at large was, at least as represented by specific individuals in Margery Kempe's story, in some sense as subjective as Kempe's own consciousness. Her *Book* gives us, for example, the monk who wished this woman who behaved so peculiarly "enclosed in a house of stone so that there no man should speak with thee" (20); the ecclesiastical clerks who insisted that "She hath a devil in her for she speaketh of the gospel" (113), and the men of the populace who continued, even after she had achieved fairly wide acceptance as a religious mystic in the world, to abjure her: "Damsel, forsake this life that thou hast, and go spin and card, as other women do, and suffer not so much shame and so much woe" (117).

Not long after the onset of her weeping, Kempe relates that she was asked to have her experiences set into a book, a request to which she could not accede unless certain that it was God's will. This certainty was some forty years coming, and it was not until much later that Dame Margery Kempe became, in a thoroughly original sense, the author of her own life.

Kempe is concerned almost from her first sentence with the power of the word, (and the Word in a spiritual sense). She must speak to her confessor if he is to pronounce her penance and absolution, and she will not. Her reason, as she presents it, is that she cannot warm to his manner. Even with the fear of death upon her, after a long and difficult birth, she refuses to speak. Although she tells her reader that the sin she does not confess is a mortal one, she nowhere in her *Book* discloses what it is, or alludes to having confessed it at some other date. While this reticence may, religiously, be both reasonable and acceptable, it is also a thoroughly effective narrative technique, a setting of the storyteller's hook, that works effectively in a spiritual autobiography devoted to the evolution of a religious consciousness marked by Kempe's peculiar gift.

The ultimate refusal of the writer to reveal her secret makes good sense if one considers the reversals of circumstance and the doubles of her own experience presented in the text, and what these reveal about Kempe's experience of words. Having begun her book with her own insanity and fear after the birth of her first child, she returns to a similar situation later on, after she has become known as a holy woman. In chapter 75, she refers to the case of a man whose wife is insane after childbirth. Doctors and priests alike have been unable to help this woman, yet when she is visited by Margery Kempe, her sanity returns, remaining with her as long as Margery does, and returning when Margery does. This circumstance (coupled with Kempe's own postpartum refusal to talk to a priest) implies that, at least in some instances, fruitful communication is not possible between men and women, may even be made impossible by the coming to fruition of their sexual congress.

Because the men on this occasion are unable to understand what the woman has to say, they have judged her insane; but her return to sanity in the presence of Margery Kempe argues that between one woman and another, communication is both possible and fruitful,--certainly an instance of that vernacular and womanly culture in which women's words are crucial-- and even that Margery Kempe is herself the bearer and restorer of sanity where the authoritarian male figures of doctor and priest have failed. Similar revisions of earlier experience follow Margery's return to England from her first pilgrimage, on which her only reliable guide had been a "broken-backed man" (*BMK* 93) provided by God, while the physically whole members of her company resorted to slander and malice where she was concerned, refusing her space at their table and, if she is to be believed, countenancing the theft of her sheets by a priest.

Having begun her pilgrimage on a tide of enthusiasm and victory over scoffers, she finds on her return that an erstwhile supporter of her vocation, has been convinced by gossip that she has borne and abandoned an illegitimate child in Europe (*BMK* 90)and that she cannot dissuade him from this belief. She faces the enmity of former friends almost everywhere, by her own account, victim of "rumors and grutching against her" (*BMK* 31) and of "much slander" (34). Only Christ's persistent reminder that he will always remember "how thou art written on my hands and feet" (*BMK* 22) and that she is a vessel of grace through which the risen God "should be crucified again by cruel words" (*BMK* 74) gives her the strength to go on. The general situation underlying the latter parts of Kempe's book is that her former supporters, moved by malicious gossip, have revised their earlier opinion of Margery Kempe, mystic, and become her accusers. Language in the world is experienced as "rumor" and "slander," while in Kempe's religious experience the language that causes her to suffer identifies her with Christ crucified;[3] words become Word when her suffering is inscribed on the body of Christ, he the tablet and she the living text.

Even her designation as a bride of Christ, also the designation of the church and of nuns, served as a powerful double of conventional feminine roles within the structure of the church. Kempe's insistence on speaking *in the world* rather than being *cloistered away from* the world that was her home does much to counter the oppressive weight of religious institutions.

To the end of the narrative, Kempe's sensitivity to power of words and the Word persists. She tells us, her weeping having declined in frequency and violence in her later years, "as some spoke evil of her before because she cried, so some spoke evil of her now because she cried not" (*BMK* 142). Of the actual writing of her treatise, Kempe tells us "she was many times sick while this treatise was in the writing, and, as soon as she would go about the writing of this treatise, she was hale and whole suddenly" (*BMK* 98) -- healed, it would seem, by the act of objectifying herself in text.

---

[3]For Kempe, as for her contemporaries, the *imitatio Christi* was a complex and multifaceted mode of worship, including such varied activities as reading, pilgrimage, and meditation (Lochrie 31) -- all of which, in one way or another, allowed the religious sensibility a means of experiencing Christ "in a region of similitude" (Lochrie 32).

The Book of Margery Kempe emerges, first, as the frame for a disruptive countertext. The intentional "surface" narrative of her spiritual advancement as a bride of Christ in the world is accomplished through the narrative of her separation from husband and children, which, sanctioned by the Church, permitted her a highly controversial freedom in behavior and utterance and second as the first autobiographical document in English to annex divine sanction for what would otherwise, at best, have been socially suspect behavior on the part of a woman. By insisting on her vocation as a free woman in the world, Kempe arrogated the authority of God to supervene the authority of Church and tradition. For Kempe, the world was organized by the medieval Catholic vision, and she had to define herself within and against that particular visionary system. Kempe's workaday world, for at least the first forty years of her life, was firmly grounded on English soil, her subsequent forays being undertaken not as voyages of emigration, but as pilgrimages from which she expected to return home, as evidenced by her prayer, ". . . spare me til I come again to England." (*BMK* 97)

Kempe, in order to define a role that encompassed what she was rather than what she was expected to be, needed to negotiate some settlement with husband, father, and church. Yet she was not completely isolated in this effort. Margery Kempe had the developing European tradition of female piety with which to identify her voice. Kempe also possessed a religious sensibility that colored her life. The central experience that legitimized Margery Kempe as an autobiographer was a religious conversion in which the Christian, touched by God's grace, experienced a transformation of emotion and belief that gave new and renewed meaning to the life of faith. Margery Kempe experienced her conversion following childbirth, turning as a result from the life of a busy wife to the life of a Catholic mystic. The resonant autobiographical voice and authority derived from the deeply emotional and deeply personal experience of God changed for her the vision of the world she inhabited and her apprehension of her place in that world.

If, as George Gusdorf suggests, ". . . the theological mirror of the

Christian soul is a deforming mirror that plays up without pity the slightest faults of the moral personality" (34), it remains, nonetheless, the only glass available to the early European women writers of autobiography. Fiction (even fiction cast in poetic form) made a difficult mode of self-disclosure, and one in which a woman who attached her name to her text risked dismissal by serious readers. The writer of letters, although she might find a considerable measure of freedom in what she said, had an audience which, while arguably a central part of her society, limited the number of her readers to the number of her correspondents. The private nature of the journal made it, in some respects, an inappropriate vehicle for the public disclosure of the self. If, however, a writing woman seized the authority of religious purpose in constructing her narrative, she placed her document in an a context that demanded consideration and went far to deny marginalization. However difficult religious discourse made the problem of writing a life that did not fit the prescribed pattern--the preconceived reflection that did not match the original image--it at least afforded a mode of disclosure that guaranteed a wider readership and a weightier consideration. It is worth noting that the reflecting glass was less kind to women than to men.

Any Christian autobiographer, engaged in the effort of structuring the narrative of his or her life, was faced with the difficulty of relating a life defined (if not valued) by its sins, which were the necessary motives for spiritual struggle. This autobiographer also faced the difficulty of not usurping the central importance in the text that should belong to God. The exercise of authorship, never easy, was made more complicated by the writer's enforced awareness that what mattered was not the writer, but the God that made the writing possible.[4]

---

[4]In his discussion of *logogic sites* (points in the literature that invite "hesitation and contemplation" {2}) in Puritan American literature, William Scheick has identified the "interweaving of the artist's craft and the Creator's artistry" (3) as a means by which the writer "could mediate authorial anxiety through his or her own art" (3). In his view, the increasing complexity of such interweaving permits greater mediatory function within the text.

However, the independence granted to men in Christian tradition -- the right to speak of weighty matters and to preach the glory of God, to participate in a public life -- made the problematic work of writing in some ways easier of execution than it was for most women. Denied such independence, the right to speak and to preach, and denied public identity, how could a woman structure the story of her own living? In the face of these denials, what weight could there be to her story? What sanctioned discourse did she have?

The obvious answer is that she had, essentially, the same discourse as the men,[5] although her relation to that discourse was somewhat different. As a consequence of her position in the social scheme, within which she occupied a constrained (and most commonly domestic) space, a woman could employ a conventional autobiographical form (as did Margery Kempe), making adjustments in the text to accommodate her own position in the social order -- to accommodate her own perceptions of and responses to life as she experienced it. Her use of language and her manipulation of the literary form at hand, not surprisingly, are not authoritative or assured in the same sense that a man's are, and the narrative she creates (or the story she has to tell) is different from the narrative of her male contemporaries.

In Margery Kempe's work, this difference reveals itself in the colloquial nature of remembered conversation, which serves to dramatize for the reader the author's position in the social layers of language[6] by demonstrating the considerable disparity between her language and the language of Christ and his earthly deputies, the priests of the Church. The text offers the reader a

---

[5]Denise Despres, in *Ghostly Sights*, expounds at some length the relationship of Kempe to the Franciscan practice of piety, an essentially masculine discourse within which the mystic could participate.

[6]For a comprehensive treatment of the types of language used in *The Book of Margery Kempe*, see Clarissa Atkinson's *Mystic and Pilgrim: the World and Book of Margery Kempe*. For a rhetorical approach to the Kempe text, see Cheryl Glenn's "Rhetorical Strategies in *The Book of Margery Kempe.*"

countertextual movement in which the overt story of spiritual advancement and submission to Christ is balanced and subverted by the story of the writer's advancement to greater competence and independence in the physical and intellectual sphere. In these textual instances, the subversive function within the text is also an act of rebellion, in which the arrogated authority of religious inspiration clothes the rebellious quality of the work in a more subdued -- and subtle -- mantle.[7]

As Kempe's text offers a beginning, it also offers a useful way of perceiving literary relationship. As the first autobiography in the English language, *The Book of Margery Kempe* might reasonably have been expected to become the cornerstone of English autobiographical tradition. In fact, it did not. Upon its completion in 1438, the manuscript disappeared from view, effectively lost to the world[8] until its rediscovery (in 1934) and publication in modernized English by William Butler-Bowden in 1936, and the subsequent 1944 publication of the manuscript in its original language by The Early English Text Society.

As it happened, Margery Kempe's name did not vanish entirely from the literary record. In 1501, extracts of her book were published in London by Wynken de Worde, and reprinted in 1521 by Henry Pepwell, both of these editions presumably reflecting contemporary taste in devotions. These published extracts consisted of her more conventional conversations with God, not one of

---

[7]It is not my purpose to suggest that any of these texts lacked genuine religious inspiration, but rather to suggest that the religious experience related in each text is inextricably tied to the mundane situation of the writer, a situation more likely to put obstacles in her path than otherwise.

[8]Although it had disappeared from general view, the manuscript was not lost utterly. As B.A. Windeatt has pointed out, the manuscript resided at the Mount Grace Priory in Yorkshire where it was annotated by readers interested in mystical experience (9). As Karma Lochrie argues, the marginalia and glossing on the manuscript appear in a late fifteenth- or early sixteenth-century hand, proving that the manuscript was being actively read within the Mount Grace community (120).

which referred to the most distinctive aspect of her vocation, her life in the world. Taken from one perspective, the de Worde and Pepwell printings represent outrageous editorial misrepresentation of Kempe's original work; from another, merely the sensible effort to salvage something of value from a renegade manuscript. The Wynken de Worde text sufficiently altered the original book that Margery Kempe came to be referred to in the Pepwell reprint as an anchoress, something which she emphatically was not.

Because Margery Kempe was, by her own assertion, illiterate, her perceived relation to her own text, as well as to the autobiographical tradition, and to the tradition of feminine piety (exemplified by Catherine of Siena, Birgitta of Sweden, Blessed Angela of Foligno, and Dorothea of Montau[9]) as it was

---

[9]Noble born St. Bridget of Sweden (1303-73), who married at thirteen, convinced her husband to spare her chastity for two years, but went on to bear him eight children. She was drawn, however, to the religious life. On the death of her husband in 1343 she entered the life of religious visionary and pilgrim, founding an order of nuns. She dictated her *Revelations*, and lived the latter portion of her life at Rome. Marie of Oignies (? - 1312), daughter of a wealthy family, was married at fourteen despite her religious vocation. She and her husband lived chastely, nursing lepers. She became a hermit in a cell at the Monastery of Oignies. She is credited with the gifts of tears, prophecy, visions and ecstasies. Angela of Foligno (1249-1309) who was a comfortably well-off wife and mother, underwent a conversion at the age of forty, subsequent to which, her family having died, she gave herself to poverty and penitence. Like Marie of Oignies, she received the gift of tears; she longed to suffer a terrible death and humiliation for the love of Christ. Her textual productions were written down by her Franciscan confessor. Dorothea of Montau (1347-94), a middle-class housewife like Kempe, was married at sixteen to an older man who mistreated her, and to whom she bore nine children of which only one lived. Eventually, the couple vowed chastity, and Dorothea embarked on a life of pilgrimage. In 1390, after her husband's death, she became a recluse under the care of John of Marienwerder, who committed to paper her life story and her visions. She also had the gift of tears. Texts in Middle English existed for the works of both Bridget of Sweden and Catherine of Siena, as well as for Mathild of Hackebourne, and were popular in the fourteenth century (Lochrie 2). It is impossible not to speculate that Kempe had encountered these texts, particularly given the current scholarship on women's literacy in medieval England.

developing on the continent, is unusual.[10] To produce a text at all, Kempe's *Book* assures us, she required the help of an amanuensis (male of course) who, because of Kempe's illiteracy, might have been able to exercise great control over the text.[11] In short, her relation to the developing autobiographical tradition of female mystics has until quite recently been perceived as that of the listener, rather than the reader; the teller rather than the writer. Her familiarity with such lives (whether they were read or heard) as that of St. Brigit of Sweden, Marie of Oignies, Angela of Foligno, and Dorothea of Montau would have depended on a general dissemination of the texts.

The recent work of scholars including Josephine Koster Tarvers, Karma Lochrie, and B.A. Windeatt,[12] however, casts Kempe's literacy in a relatively problematic light. Tarvers points to the unfortunate, but thoroughly understandable, critical reluctance to "search the numerous didactic and exegetical texts which survive, often obscurely catalogued, in manuscript" (307) because of firmly entrenched canonical expectations regarding female literacy. She then asserts that a less biased assessment of surviving texts yield evidence that "women

---

[10]Of these women, Kempe refers repeatedly to Brigit (or St. Bride) in a manner that Windeatt suggests proves "how potent a model the English woman found for herself in the life and revelations of the visionary Swedish saint"(17), who also employed an amanuensis.

[11]The garrulous voice of *The Book of Margery Kempe*, however, is so consistent, and so insistent on telling the story in its own discursive fashion, that it seems unlikely that the scribe edited the text to any great extent. Kempe's apparent control of the text has also been noted by Karma Lochrie, who cites Kempe's apology for her scribe's faulty recollection of the story of Marie of Oignies (119). Karma Lochrie and B.A. Windeatt both note Kempe's use of Latin as it echoes Richard Rolle as an indication that she may, in fact, have known some Latin.

[12]M.B. Parkes' 1973 essay, "The Literacy of the Laity," presents the literacy dispute with regard to medieval women with great thoroughness, advancing the view that the illiteracy of women consisted of a decline in the knowledge of French and Latin, rather than of general illiteracy as the term is generally understood today.

wrote both complete works and letters, and copied or had them copied, considered them their property. . . ."(307) and that women, though probably to a lesser extent than men, "participated in the learned community" (307). She also points out that Kempe's use of an amanuensis may have been "a function of her social status" (308) rather than of her ignorance. In the same general vein, Karma Lochrie reminds us that "illiteracy in the Middle Ages is not the same as illiteracy today" (101), since literacy, in medieval usage, referred to "the ability to read, but not necessarily to write, Latin," (101) and that "women were increasingly literate [but not necessarily able to write] in the vernacular" (103).

Windeatt and Lochrie have both noted the Latinity of the Kempe text, suggesting that she might, in fact, have known some Latin. Windeatt, in particular, cites another problem toward the end of Book I of Kempe's *Book*. Here, Christ tells the author:

> I have often said unto you that whether you pray with your mouth
> or think with your heart, whether you read or hear reading, I will
> be pleased with you. (*BMK* 218)

In Windeatt's reading, this wording suggests that Kempe could very well have been capable of reading, as well as of hearing things read.

Consequently, while it can be said that *The Book of Margery Kempe* took place in a developing tradition--and not at the absolute margins of that tradition and the larger society of which it was a part--its place in that tradition is anomalous. There is no absolute certainty regarding Kempe's literacy or illiteracy. To further complicate matters, Kempe's position as a female mystic may well have enforced, at the least, a posture of illiteracy on her part. The female mystic had no assured right to expression (Lochrie 79,80). In fact, Lochrie attests, the prescribed religious life for a woman consisted for the most part "in adopting boundaries and maintaining an unbroken body" (24). In other words, she was expected to maintain a hermetic silence that would preserve her from speech (or other interaction) with the world, from discourse or intercourse that would "diffuse one's relation with God" (25).[13]   Thus, the validating principal of Kempe's text had to be not that she spoke, but that Christ spoke through her.   Nor is it my purpose to impose a purely secular vision on the reading of the text; in the words of Denise Despres, "Unless we deny Margery's credibility altogether--and some of the most powerful men and women of her day did not--we must accept the fact that she possessed powers of vision generally outside our everyday experience." (60)   There is an irony here, to Windeatt's belief that Kempe "would probably not have believed that human experience was worth recording for its own sake" (22), for it is *her* voice, "human speech itself which continuously catches and sharpens the attention. . ."(22).

The Book of Margery Kempe is the written record of a soul's journey to harmony with God; that is, in Christian terms, the willed submission to God's will. Thus, the choice for Kempe was not whether to submit or be independent, but rather the choice of which master to serve. Her ability to exercise this choice, however, depended on her ability to secure from her husband his guarantee (as it was given in their vow of chastity before the Bishop of Lincoln), and then to secure the endorsement of the church itself.

Because the spiritual journey is generally conceived as in some measure separate from the empirical journey of the body, the text of a spiritual autobiography need not be overly concerned with the externals of an individual life. Consequently, Margery Kempe was able to produce an autobiography that recorded most intently her inner religious life, beginning at about her twenty-first year with the birth of her first child. Whatever occurred before that date, the narrative implies, is of no consequence. Yet reason suggests that the earlier life which formed her for her religious vocation must itself have some value or meaning, as must the fourteen children she bore John Kempe in the interim

---

[13] A detailed and well supported explanation of the place of the female body in medieval theology and thought appears in Lochrie's *Margery Kempe and Translations of the Flesh.*

between her first dialogue with Christ and the day when she and her husband took their mutual vow of chastity and commenced to live apart. Yet these children are never named in the narrative, and no explanation is given of how they were cared for. In leaving this information out of her narrative, Kempe continues a practice already common in the narratives of continental female mystics--her knowledge of which argues an immersion in a significant level of the religious culture of her day. By choosing to exclude from her narrative the events preceding her discovery of vocation, as well as her very real day-to-day life as a wife and mother, Kempe denies those definitions of woman that would keep her at her society's outer edges.

In view of Kempe's choices as a narrator of what not to tell, it is worth noting again Clarissa Atkinson's speculation that her father's death provided not only the requisite money to pay her own and her husband's debts, but also the psychological liberty she needed to begin her pilgrimage to the Holy Land (Atkinson, 4).[14] The external aspects of her life, or at any rate those she chooses to relate, are largely divorced from the personal context dictated by the idea of a woman's proper sphere of existence (a sphere defined and ruled over by men), dealing not with house, husband, and children but with those men of the church who supported or denied her vocation, and her fellow lay persons, citizens and pilgrims both, who were often bitterly divided as to the genuineness of her calling.

Like all writers, Kempe has chosen not only what not to tell, but what to tell; like all writers, she is sometimes betrayed by her text into revealing what she probably intended to conceal. Her intention "was to tell of God's dealing with her soul" (Cholmeley 42). At the same time, as Atkinson points out, "To recognize an author's stated intention is not to preclude all other motivations" (7).

---

[14]Indeed, since she had apparently married beneath her father's status in Bishop's Lynn, the is some likelihood that her inheritance on her father's death restored her to an earlier level of prestige.

Thus the story of her relationship with Christ, a tale she intends as a vindication of the life for which she says she was chosen, also is the tale of her life in the world, a life that she chose to pursue against tremendous opposition, her conversion having marked only the beginning of a struggle that continued for the rest of her life. It is also the story of a woman who was denied the language she needed (barred as she was from preaching, and, she would have us believe, from knowledge of the written word) and who nonetheless insisted on being heard.

The nature of her gift, which is certainly an expressive, emotive form of communication (or disruption), coupled with her first refusal to speak[15] and her later refusal to disclose the sin behind the refusal, suggests that her text performs two simultaneous functions. It stands not only as her affirmation and vindication of her own religious vocation, and of the life in the world that her specific vocation dictated, but as her disruption of and challenge to the discourse of her day, a discourse to which she was denied participatory access by conventional means. Her weeping, for example, had so disrupted the friar's discourse within the church that only her removal would satisfy him. That same weeping, once it was recognized as a holy gift, enabled her to speak of Christ to others with relative impunity, and finally to have her words inscribed by a friar, material evidence that her gift had given her the power to determine what a churchman might commit to paper. Her autobiography, laboriously dictated to her priestly scribes, remains as the ambivalent testimony to her extreme determination that her voice not be silenced or lost. The enduring presence of that voice suggests that Margery Kempe, despite the forces of faith and convention, was (and

---

[15]The refusal to speak, coupled with the writer's initial reluctance to put her life into a book, reveal willed silences on the author's part that are as expressive as her speech, since she is fully in control of her silence and can use it to make known her will. Similarly, Kempe's exclusion from the text of much of her experience as a wife and mother is yet another powerful and expressive use of silence. That Kempe had almost definitely absorbed this particular narrative practice from the published lives of other female mystics in no way lessens its effect.

remains) part of a vigorous current of literary development that is not, after all, utterly separate from the main stream.

WORKS CITED

Atkinson, Clarissa L. *Mystic and Pilgrim: The Book and the World of Margery Kempe*. Ithaca: Cornell University Press, 1983.

Cholmeley, Katharine. *Margery Kempe, Genius And Mystic*. New York: Longmans, Green & Co., 1947.

Dame Julian of Norwich. Excerpts from *A Book of Showings*. in *The Norton Anthology of Literature by Women*. ed. Sandra M. Gilbert and Susan Gubar. New York: W.W. Norton, 1985.

Despres, Denise. *Ghostly Sights*. Norman, OK: Pilgrim Books, 1989.

Glenn, Cheryl. "Rhetorical Strategy in *The Book of Margery Kempe*." *College English*. Vol. 54, #5, Sept. '92. (540-554)

Gusdorf, George. "Conditions and Limits of Autobiography." in *Autobiography, Essays Theoretical and Critical*. ed. James Olney. Princeton: Princeton University Press, 1980.

Lochrie, Karma. *Margery Kempe and Translations of the Flesh*. USA: U. of Pennsylvania Press, 1991.

Parkes, M.B. "The Literacy of the Laity." *The Medieval World*. Ed. David Daiches and Anthony Thorlby. London: Aldus, 1973.

Tarvers, Josephine Koster. "'thys ys my mystrys boke': English Women as Readers and Writers in Late Medieval England." *The Uses of Manuscripts in Literary Studies*. USA: Western Michigan University, Medieval Institute Publications, 1992.

Windeatt, B.A. "Introduction" to the *Book of Margery Kempe*. NY: Penguin, 1988.

Seventeenth-Century Spiritual Autobiography:
Paul's Epistles and John Bunyan's
Grace Abounding to the Chief of Sinners

Joseph Zornado

Yale Divinity School

Most scholars agree that seventeenth-century English spiritual autobiography reaches its zenith in John Bunyan's *Grace Abounding to the Chief of Sinners,* a text that demonstrated remarkable influence and longevity of appeal. Exactly how momentous a *literary* achievement this is, however, does not garner the same critical like-mindedness (Shumaker). Bunyan's autobiography, as well his best-known work, *The Pilgrim's Progress,* have been derided as examples of Bunyan's literary sensibility, which is seen by some as common, vulgar, and given to excess. Still, the debate over the quality of *Grace Abounding's* literary sensibility notwithstanding, the text was part and parcel of a literary movement wildly popular in the seventeenth century.

Margaret Bottrall states that one researcher, a Mr. York Tindall, "claims to have read no fewer than two thousand tracts by seventeenth-century lay-preachers, their friends and enemies, and [that] he has succeeded in proving with a wealth of evidence that *Grace Abounding* belongs to an accepted genre" (86). As Bottrall's study reveals, whether or not Bunyan's spiritual autobiography and others like it were "vulgar" or "common," spiritual autobiography had widespread acceptance, and was a well-known genre for seventeenth-century readers. Given the popularity of the genre, and of Bunyan's text in particular, an intriguing question is whether Bunyan relied on a pretext (in the sense of pre-existing text) to lend shape and depth to his spiritual autobiography, or whether he "invented" the genre as he went.

One might first assume that Augustine's long, influential shadow fell across Bunyan. Yet Linda Peterson's 1988 study, "Newman's *Apologia pro vita sua* and the Traditions of the English Spiritual Autobiography," argues that Augustine's confessions play little or no role in the development of seventeenth-century English spiritual autobiography. Furthermore, Peterson asserts in this essay that Bunyan's own work served as the pretext for the thousands of spiritual autobiographies that followed. I would like to suggest that Bunyan's own spiritual journey described in *Grace Abounding to the Chief of Sinners* reveals the influence of New Testament epistolary writings, specifically the biographical information scattered among the book of Acts and the epistles written by, and about, Paul the Apostle. From *Grace Abounding's* Pauline-styled prefatory remarks, to the Pauline allusion in the title of the work, to the now familiar form of seventeenth-century spiritual autobiography, ample evidence reveals that Paul's epistles served as pretext for Bunyan's own spiritual autobiography, and countless other seventeenth-century spiritual autobiographer who, by adopting the "Bunyanesque" style, subsumed Paul's influence into their own texts.

Linda Peterson, whose study of Newman's *Apologia pro vita sua* traces the traditions of English Spiritual Autobiography "from Bunyan through Newton, Cowper, and Scott" (Peterson 304), reaffirms the critical appraisals of years past: English spiritual autobiography had a recognizable, predictable form that writers employed, at least until Newman's highly influential secular autobiography appeared (309). In her study, Peterson makes clear the distinction between seventeenth-century spiritual autobiography--the "Bunyanesque patterns and form"--and Newman's nineteenth-century secular autobiography, *Apologia*. Newman's text, Peterson discovers, imitates for the first time Augustine's

Confessions rather than Bunyan's *Grace Abounding*. Peterson remarks that:

> Augustine's *Confessions* has frequently been cited as a seminal
> work in the tradition of spiritual autobiography, but in the English
> tradition before Newman its formal influence was, in fact
> negligible. . . .and it was Newman, too, who through the *Apologia*
> reminded English autobiographers of the Augustinian figures and
> form they might use as alternatives to Bunyanesque patterns. (309)

By 1865, then, when Newman's autobiography was published as a book,
spiritual autobiography had already been influenced through and through by the
patterns and form of Bunyan's *Grace Abounding*, so much so that Bunyan's form
had become the touchstone for autobiography throughout the second half of the
seventeenth century: autobiographers either deliberately imitated or, in a posture
that came later with Newman, consciously avoided the "Bunyanesque patterns"
in writing their life histories.

Peterson implicitly suggests that autobiography springs from two different
sources: Bunyan and Augustine. It seems clear from Peterson's argument that
Newman rejected the Bunyanesque patterns and form of seventeenth-century
spiritual autobiography, favoring Augustine's more personal, more historical
attempt at interpreting his own "living experience" (300). At least one
unanswered question arises at this point. If not Augustine, then who influenced
Bunyan, and the thousands of seventeenth-century autobiographers? Answers to
this question may range form the nebulous "church fathers" to "the Acts of the
Apostles," but none of these answers are specific. Certainly Bunyan was not the
first spiritual autobiographer--though at time critics seem to suggest, as Peterson
does, by not addressing this question, that seventeenth-century spiritual
autobiography sprang from the head of John Bunyan fully formed.

That Bunyan was not the first spiritual autobiographer seems an obvious
point--but it is a point overlooked consistently enough to bear reiteration. In fact,
some critics betray a remarkable misunderstanding of Bunyan's *Grace Abounding*
because of their failure to recognize the pretext that guided Bunyan's
autobiography. In G.A. Starr's *Defoe and Spiritual Autobiography,* for instance,

he makes only a passing reference to Bunyan and his work, choosing to concentrate on later writers as examples of seventeenth-century spiritual autobiography.

Appraising James Fraser of Brae, Starr claims:

> Fraser's zeal is moderated by a sense of decorum. He does not strain to appear monstrously sinful before conversion, or exceptionally sanctified afterward: glorifying God, he does not covertly glorify himself. The lyrical ejaculations of men like Bunyan are deservedly well known, less familiarly, however, are the writings of men like Fraser who allow themselves no such license. (39)

And further on Starr again betrays his misreading of Bunyan, (and the Christian gospel) when he states that,"one gets few glimpses of [Fraser's] actual transgressions, which in any case were too mild and infrequent to earn him any Bunyanesque title to having been the chief of sinners" (46). Margaret Bottrall makes the same mistake. She writes that

> *Grace Abounding the Chief of Sinners* is the most poignantly personal of all the autobiographical studies produced in seventeenth-century England; yet its very title, emotionally extravagant as it is, provokes the question, how far is it trustworthy as a record of experience? (85)

Starr and Bottrall question the trustworthiness of Bunyan's *Grace Abounding* for the same reason--they misread its title. The Apostle Paul's conversion narrative--and Bunyan's self-conscious imitation of it in *Grace Abounding*--suggest that the snatches of spiritual autobiography found in Paul's New Testament epistles provide the basic format for Bunyan (and countless others). With this in mind, Starr's and Bottrall's criticism of Bunyan as an overly zealous Christian prone to "lyrical ejaculations" and overblown claims in regards to his sinfulness undermines itself, revealing more about their misunderstanding of Christian doctrine than about their understanding of Bunyan and *Grace Abounding*.

Bunyan begins his autobiography with a preface that clearly echoes the introductory greetings in Paul's epistles:

Children, Grace be with you, Amen. I being taken from you in presence, and so tied up, that I cannot perform that duty that from God do lie upon me, to you-ward, for your further edifying and building up in Faith and Holiness, &c., yet that you may see my soul hath fatherly care and desire after your spiritual and everlasting welfare. . .I do look yet after you all, greatly longing to see your safe arrival in THE desired heaven.

I thank God upon every Remembrance of you, and rejoyce even while I stick between the Teeth of the Lions in the Wilderness, at the grace, and mercy, and knowledge of Christ our saviour, which God hath bestowed upon you, with an abundance of Faith and Love. (1)

Bunyan comes very near to quoting Paul's distinct style of greeting in the first line of the above preface, "Grace with you all, Amen." Further, Bunyan's explanation of his absence again echoes Paul's own apologies for his absence. Both men, coincidently, wrote to their brethren from prison; both men accepted imprisonment as a consequence of preaching the truth to a deceived population. Surely Bunyan did not overlook the most remarkable parallel between himself and the apostle Paul: each wrote the bulk of his spiritual autobiography from a prison cell, separated from his brethren by a government unsympathetic to the "truth" (Romans 1.13).

Similar rhetorical styles further reflect Paul's influence on Bunyan's work. Bunyan's introductory rhetoric functions almost as a collection of Paul's separate salutations in his own epistles. In 1 Corinthians, 1:4, Paul writes, "I thank my God always concerning you, for the grace of God which was given you in Christ Jesus." And in Paul's letter to the Philippians he writes, "I thank my God in all my remembrance of you, always offering prayer with joy in my every prayer for you all: (1: 3-4). In his letter to Philemon Paul directly refers to his own imprisonment:

therefore, though I have enough confidence in Christ to order to do that which is proper, yet for love's sake I rather appeal to you-- since I am such a person as Paul, the aged, and now also a prisoner of Christ Jesus--I appeal to you for my child, whom I have begotten in my *imprisonment*, Onesiumus. (1: 8-0) (Italics mine.)

I cite this passage only to draw attention to what surely Bunyan was aware of: both he and Paul were prisoner for [and of] Christ, sacrificing all for their faith. This was certainly not lost on Bunyan Though Bunyan only alludes to his own imprisonment, he too was jailed, and he too spent his time writing to edify his flock, and he too, when released periodically, continued to preach, though breaking the law and risking further punishment. Bunyan did manage to extend a six-month term into twelve years for his crimes of holding a conventicle. Paul, of course, was beheaded for his preaching, the merciful alternative to crucifixion accorded to Roman citizens.

Though Bunyan's preface self-consciously imitates Paul's epistolary greetings, a far more significant similarity exists between the two spiritual autobiographies: critical moments in the individual life suffering conversion appear to others as spiritually insignificant if not non-existent. Spiritual crisis occurs because an event provides insight into an individual's corrupt state. The event, finally, has no bearing at all on the depth of the spiritual experience. For instance, insignificant events--listening to bells as a pastime--produced the most profound *internal* acts of contrition for Bunyan. As an adult, Bunyan was castigated by his own conscience. A spirit of contrition, or even of neurotic guilt, does not require overt acts of "sin" to induce it. Certainly Paul appears to have committed the most grievous crimes before his conversion--*i.e.* hunting down the church in support of his own Hebraic Law. Nevertheless, Paul withdrew into the desert for fourteen years after his experience on the road to Damascus. And in all this time the "thorn" in his side, an internal, emotional affliction rather than a physical one, never left Paul. In short, Paul's version of the gospel focused on the sinner's unrepentant and sinful heart, not his actions, deeds, or visible sins.

To hierarchize sins into "bad" and "worse" reflected a ludicrous and prideful notion for Paul and Bunyan. And on this point Starr and Bottrall again misread Bunyan, not recognizing the influence of Paul's gospel to the Gentiles. For Starr, Bunyan's sins were "insignificant," and not enough to warrant the grandiose title, "chief of sinners." Similarly, Bottrall states that Bunyan seems to have had no normal standards of reference by which to judge the heinousness of his offenses" (108). This raises a question. Just what defines a "normal" standard of reference? Do the apostles also lack a "normal" standard of reference? Both Bottrall and Starr are guilty of some of the pride and smugness they attribute to Bunyan. "Normal" in this case sheds more light on Bottrall's own anxiety regarding Bunyan's commitment to his beliefs than it does on Bunyan's state of mind. That Bunyan was troubled by his sinful thoughts, regardless of his actual behavior, suggests that Bunyan had his own "standard of reference," though it may not appear "normal" to various late twentieth-century readers. Bunyan's "standard of reference," aside from the Calvinistic demands his beliefs placed on his conscience, were set by Paul's example.

In 1 Timothy 1: 14-15, Paul writes:

> and the grace of our Lord was more than abundant, with the faith and love which are found in Christ Jesus. It is a trustworthy statement, deserving full acceptance, that Christ Jesus came into the world to save sinners, *among whom I am foremost of all.* (Italics mine.)

Paul considered himself the "chief" of sinners, even as he spread Christianity's influence throughout the Roman world. Let there be no mistake, Paul does not consider himself the "foremost" of all sinners because of what he has done in the past, but because of his sinful nature *as a fallen man. Grace Abounding to the Chief of Sinners* draws a direct parallel to Paul's gospel to the gentiles, and to Paul's own spiritual autobiography. Bunyan understood that the love Christ preached extended even to the chief of sinners. The appeal of his autobiography--an his other writings--undoubtedly hinged on this point.

The seventeenth century quite possibly responds to Bunyan in part due to the recognition of a soul truly struggling with itself and its maker. More importantly, Bunyan's autobiography of a life *so* undramatic and so mundane allows his readers to identify their own mundane, undramatic lives as potentially sinful, and to ask: if Bunyan could be the chief of sinners, what of me?

Bunyan's spiritual autobiography provides the realization that grace abounds not only to author, but in the true spirit of Paul's gospel to the gentiles, grace abounds to the reader. In other words, like Paul's epistles, Bunyan's work implicitly invites his audience to identify Bunyan's life as exemplary, even as Bunyan identified Paul's life as exemplary. The autobiography, then, whether consciously or not, elegantly taps into the need to hierarchize sin, causing the readers to find themselves wanting in comparison to Bunyan's commitment to God and ultimately, causing the readers to find themselves "chief of sinners" in their own right. Finally, grace will cover all--and Bunyan and his audience are saved.

Whether Bunyan intended it or not, his conversion narrative associates itself with Paul's. Though Bunyan's sins were not graphic crimes against humanity, *i.e.* they did not appear to be "abnormal" behavior according to Bottrall's moral rating scale, when compared to Christ, and *when compared to Paul*, Bunyan finds himself utterly fallen. For Bunyan to claim anything less would be to reject the Pauline gospel--and to, in effect, raise himself above Paul For if Paul considers himself to be the chief of sinners, how can Bunyan, looking back on one the most successful Christian evangelists, consider himself anything more? The title of Bunyan's work is not an attempt at self-aggrandizement or spiritual hyperbole, as Starr implies, nor is it the product of an errant, hyper-religious man influenced by a long-past hyper-religious seventeenth century, as Bottrall would suggest. In a profound sense, the title contains the spirit of the New Testament in miniature. *Grace Abounding to the Chief of Sinners* paraphrases 1 Timothy 1:15, a passage that reminds the reader of Paul, his conversion, his ministry, and his faith, while at the same time suggesting Bunyan's own claim to the Pauline gospel of death of the flesh--that the flesh can do nothing to win salvation for itself, so that all of his readers might recognize themselves as the chief of sinners, not as a form of prideful humility, but as an encouragement to recognize and renounce one's corrupt, fallen nature and accept he abounding grace offered to all by Christ. The title of Bunyan's narrative does not ask the reader to examine the author, (though Starr and Bottrall suggest otherwise) but to examine the process of grace, and to examine that process at work in themselves.

Searching for one-to-one correspondences between the lives of Paul and Bunyan remains, of course, futile. As Christ taught, it is not the letter of the law but the spirit of the law that carries the greatest significance, and so too in the relationship between the Apostle Paul and Bunyan. Reading their respective autobiographies for similarities in theme and event involved in spiritual journey reveals the debt Bunyan--and spiritual autobiography on the whole--owes to Paul. I use the term "autobiography" loosely when referring to Paul's writing. I do not assume that he intended to pen his own spiritual life story. Yet even though his intent was to teach, and he used his life constantly as an example form which to draw, with some diligence, a creative reader can piece together Paul's spiritual autobiography from his epistles and the book of Acts.

Roger Sharrock's introduction to *Grace Abounding* outlines the fundamental form taken by nearly all spiritual autobiography during the seventeenth century. Sharrock writes that, "Bunyan and his like, socially inferior to the Presbyterian and Independent clergy and without formal education for the ministry, attempted to justify themselves and to establish their special calling by detailed accounts of the work of grace upon their souls" (xxix) Sharrock shows that the common form of spiritual autobiography showed that the spiritual life of the Christian was divided into five categories:

1) early providential mercies and opportunities
2) unregenerate life: sin and resistance to the gospel
3) conversion, often ushered in by an "awakening" sermon
4) calling: vocation to preach the Gospel and oftentimes
5) an account of the ministry, often with anecdotes to illustrate pastoral work. (xxix)

All five of these categories employed by seventeenth-century spiritual autobiographers were adapted from Paul's spiritual autobiography. Paul writes in his epistle to the Romans, Galatians, and the Phillippians brief snatches of spiritual autobiography that give an outline of his spiritual journey, a spiritual journey that appears remarkably similar to the format seventeenth-century spiritual autobiography was ultimately to adapt and exploit. In Phillippians, Chapter 3, Paul recounts his own early providential mercies and opportunities. He was deeply involved in the religion of his time and place, "circumcised the eighth day, of the nation of Israel, of the tribe of Benjamin, a Hebrew of Hebrews; as the Law, a Pharisee." As Paul goes on to explain in Galatians, the Law was a form of God's providence, being a tutor to lead him to Christ, but he rejected the opportunity. Instead, he led an unregenerate life of sin and resistance to the Gospel, and as Saul, was a chief "persecutor of Christ." Finally God struck Saul down on the road to Damascus and Christ, according to the book of Acts, spoke to Saul. As Bottrall points out, Saul at this point has a "blinding" experience and accepts the grace of Christ, and like Bunyan centuries later, he struggles for years with his new knowledge.

Paul does not ride into the Roman world immediately to preach the gospel. In fact, he wrestles with his conversion, withdrawing to Arabia, returning after three years, and withdrawing and "after an interval of fourteen years I went up again to Jerusalem." Only then did Paul's three missionary journeys take place (Galatians 2). After returning to Jerusalem, Paul confirmed his calling to preach the Gospel to the Gentiles, having feared until that time that he might be "running in vain." The apostles in Jerusalem approved of Paul's preaching and sent him out. My point is this: Paul grew into the role of "Church father" by the "merciful working of God upon [his] soul (Bunyan 1). Neither Paul nor Bunyan were "promoted" instantaneously--both conversion accounts retell in one fashion or another the slow process of God's grace changing an individual's life. The conversion process that Paul lives through--and writes about--sets the standard for all conversion experiences. His spiritual conversion functions typologically, like Christian from *Pilgrim's Progress*, forging both historically and spiritually a path that an individual devoted to Christ must walk. Paul's conversion tells the story of a man's struggle to incorporate his conversion into his life: that is, to renounce his life in order to accept the call of conversion.

Bunyan organizes his autobiography according to temporal and thematic events in his spiritual journey relating one thing they have in common: their effects on his inner spirit. Unlike Saul's experience on the road to Damascus, Bunyan's experience on the streets of Bedford--his guilt of bell ringing, the brief snatches of conversation heard from the elderly women speaking of Christianity, seem undramatic. Nevertheless, from an internal perspective, Bunyan's conversion experience--his own illness, his own physical and spiritual struggle, reflect Saul's more overtly dramatic experience. Starr actually points out that:

> all Christians shared the same spiritual purpose and plight; nor was their likeness confined to a vague overall identity of predicament. More specifically, their souls underwent identical stages of development: between one spiritual pilgrimage and another, the course of successes and setbacks varied considerably in intensity but remarkably little in sequence. (38)

Even with this in mind, Starr and many other critics including Sharrock, Peterson, Shumaker, and Bottrall do not recognize the influence Paul's spiritual journey had on Bunyan's autobiography. In fact, Bottrall misses the point entirely when she states, "conversion had been, for Bunyan, no sudden blinding illumination, but a difficult, wearying, long-drawn-out process," alluding to Paul's conversion as if it had been short, simple, and easy. Bunyan's debt to Paul lies not in the specific historical similarities between their two lives--though some do exist--but in the "overall identity of predicament" both men shared (Bottrall 19).

Bottrall suggests that Paul's conversion resulted in a kind of immediate elevation to sainthood. This, of course, is not true. It is easy to confuse Paul's experience on the road to Damascus with his self-imposed exile to the solitude of the desert in which he reconciled his Hebraic teaching with his Christian revelations; the experience on the road to Damascus took only an instant, but he formation of Paul's theological and epistemological sensibility took about fourteen years. Bunyan wrestled for years with his calling as well. From the time he heard "three or four women sitting at a door in the sun, talking about the things of God" in section 37 of his autobiography, to his own tentative acceptance of his calling (concluded in section 252), Bunyan agonized over the Christian doctrine of grace and forgiveness. Clearly, Bunyan struggled for years in order to come to terms with what he understood as God's call upon his life--and he devotes nearly two-thirds of the autobiography to this part of his internal spiritual struggle. Bunyan's conversion narrative outlines the process that begins when God comes calling, whether on the road to Damascus or on a street in Bedford: it will be intense, it will be internalized, and it will take time--three elements that characterize the "Bunyanesque" style of spiritual autobiography, and Paul's own life.

Bunyan's own spiritual journey descried in *Grace Abounding to the Chief of Sinners* relies on Paul's epistles--and his version of the Gospel--as an autobiographical and theological pretext. Paul's epistles served as a kind of ur-text for Bunyan, and later for countless other seventeenth-century spiritual autobiographers who adopted the "Bunyanesque" style. This means, of course, that the lines mapping the development of seventeenth-century spiritual and secular autobiography do not run only to Bunyan or Augustine, but rather, the lines mapping autobiography precede both men. In the case of the "Bunyanesque" style of spiritual autobiography, one line runs directly to the Apostle Paul's inchoate example of epistolary spiritual autobiography.

Another question about the formal structures of seventeenth-century autobiography arises: Despite the apparent difference between Augustine's text and Bunyan's, was Augustine equally influenced by Paul's spiritual conversion and its retelling in the New Testament? If Augustine was indeed influenced by Paul's epistles and the rhetorical flourish with which he responded to early church needs, then can both spiritual and secular autobiography trace their lineage back to one source? The idea of Paul's New Testament epistles as pretext for spiritual, and later, secular autobiography does not seem all that far-fetched. The radical value that was posited in the individual by seventeenth-century Christianity, and the commensurate importance of the individual's own internal spiritual condition-- while at the same time emphasizing the universal condition of all human kind-- make up the literary sensibility necessary in undertaking autobiography for a mass readership. Bunyan's literary sensibility, though deemed crude by some, combines his own individual struggle with what he defined as sinful thoughts, with the universal need for love, acceptance, and self-understanding--all of which goes a long way towards explaining popularity of the seventeenth-century spiritual autobiography and the seminal influence of John Bunyan.

WORKS CITED

Bottrall, Margaret. *Every Man a Phoenix: Studies in Seventeenth-Century Autobiography.* London: Clowes, 1958.

The New Oxford Annotated Bible. Ed. Herbert G. May and Bruce M. Metzger. New York: Oxford UP, 1961.

Peterson, Linda. "Newman's *Apologia pro vita sua* and the Traditions of the English Spiritual Autobiography: PMLA 103 (1988): 300-314.

Sharrock, Roger. Introduction. *Grace Abounding to the Chief of Sinners.* By John Bunyan. London: Clowes, 19958.

Shumaker, Wayne. *English Autobiography: Its Emergence, Materials, and Form.* Berkeley: California UP, 1976.

Creating and Containing: Scriptural Uses in Two Early American Captivity Narratives

Karen S. Nulton

American captivity narratives merge the genres of spiritual narrative and war literature in a deft and fascinating way that is particularly significant when the narrator is a woman. The convergence of these genres within the narratives of Mary White Rowlandson and Hannah Dustan discloses much about scriptural usage and women's views of war while simultaneously dramatizing the power of the narration itself.

Had Mary White Rowlandson not written the first American captivity narrative, we would know nothing of her life. Rowlandson, who was captured by a group of Narragansett Indians during King Philip's War (and ransomed eleven weeks later to her husband), finds in her captivity the basis for a narrative of moral and spiritual growth. She also, almost incidentally, discovers something more: the voice of a Puritan woman living almost completely free of the confines of Puritan society. That Rowlandson's lives as captive and Puritan clash is inevitable; that she mediates this clash with alternating apologia and fury dramatizes the ongoing dilemma of American literary women whose lives are private yet whose words are public.

What we know of Hannah Dustan is, also, derived mainly form her captivity narrative; but what we know of her could not be more different than what we know of Mary Rowlandson. Twenty-two years after Mary Rowlandson's

capture at the hands of the Narragansetts, Dustan faces a similar ordeal. Like
Rowlandson, she sees her child killed and is taken captive by people she
perceives as hostile savages. Dustan, however, does not wait to be rescued, but
rather takes vengeance into her own--bloodied and capable--hands. Her story,
moreover, is filtered through the agendas of Cotton Mather, her editor and quasi-
biographer.[1] Because of this, if Rowlandson's narrative is one of personal
growth, Dustan's becomes one of depersonalization and containment as it is told
by Mather.

My discussion of Rowlandson and Dustan yokes three seemingly disparate
narrative genres: spiritual or conversion, captivity, and war. The most obvious
tie between captivity and spiritual narratives is that both narratives, as Daniel
Shea argues, are "primarily concerned with the question of grace" (xi). Indeed,
captivity narratives are, in many ways, simply spiritual narratives written for a
secular audience. In a compelling backflip, captivity narratives transform the
internal struggle for redemption revealed in spiritual narratives into a captive's
actual, physical struggle for redemption, and then allegorize this experience to a
spiritual level. Like Anne Bradstreet's classic text in which, though her "heart
rose" at the first sight of her new home, she declares God as her comforter and
savior, so captivity narratives such as Rowlandson's take as their immediate
raison d'etre the desire to prove God's willingness to succor and (eventually)
rescue true believers from physical and moral dangers. In this way, the message
of spiritual narratives, written to a body of known believers, is delivered to the
secular world through the drama of the captivity tale--a drama that not devoid of
a certain quasi-voyeuristic appeal.

But captivity narratives are not simply dramatic spiritual lessons.
Essentially accounts of prisoners of war, they also comprise the first body of

---

[1]To be sure, Rowlandson's tale was almost certainly filtered through the
ministerial vision of her husband, but at least she was able to write it herself, and
in the writing to reveal much about her own state of mind.

American war literature--a body written, interestingly enough, from a stereotypically female perspective. Captivity narratives, declaring both the weakness of the unempowered (or in the case of such male writers as John Williams, disempowered) and the strength and freedom offered by unconventional situations, offer a classic distillation of women's war themes regardless of the author's gender.[2]

Traditionally--and paradoxically, considering the very masculine agenda of most war literature--writing about war has freed women from many common constraints associated with the female voice. Searching for their own *personal* relationships to war (How did I become involved in this war? Who am I when I am neither a wife nor a mother? Who am I outside of the community that formed me?), women implicitly question the broader relationship of women to war. Historically, "Because women are *exterior* to war, men *interior*, men have long been the great war-story tellers, legitimated in that role because they have 'been there' or because they have greater entree into what it 'must be like,'" (*Women and War* 212). Since this construction reduces women to mere onlookers *to* war rather than participants *in* war, their war literature is often characterized as secondary in importance to men's war texts. Captivity narratives, however, place women squarely in the center of the Indian wars. That women's place in war is considered mainly within a moral and spiritual framework (and that the women are involved so very obviously against their will) helps to explain why these accounts were eagerly accepted by early American audiences, even while their analysis of war links them as firmly to Gertrude Stein's "The Winner Loses" and John Dos Passos' *Three Soldiers* as it does to spiritual autobiography.

Given the extent to which Puritan women were expected to maintain silence within their own community, it is not surprising that Rowlandson needed

---

[2]A recurring insistence in women's war texts is that, however horrible the war itself, wartime grants women significant freedom from the constraints of traditional gender roles. For a more in-depth discussion, see Karen Nulton, *The Social Civil War*. Unpublished Ph.D. dissertation: Rutgers University, 1992.

54

a protective layering of justification before she could publish her tale: similar to other women who write about their war experiences, she remains decorously silent about her everyday existence within her community while expounding at length upon her time outside of normal society. Her narrative, *The Sovereignty and Goodness of God, Together With the Faithfulness of His Promises Displayed; Being a Narrative of the Captivity and Restoration of Mrs. Mary Rowlandson. Commended by her, to all that Desires to know the Lords Doings to, and Dealing With Her*, posits her experiences first on a religious plane; only after her readers have been shown "The Sovereignty and Goodness of God" is the author willing to reveal the "Captivity and Restoration" of Mary White Rowlandson herself. Rowlandson explains that she wrote her tale "for Her Private Use," and continues that she only made it public at the behest of friends in the hope that her tale of Christian redemption, as evidenced by her trials in the wilderness and ultimate ransoming to her own people, might "declare the works of the Lord" (42). Rowlandson fulsomely assures her reader that she offers her tale only with womanly reticence and humility.

Further, as Amy Shrager Lang points out, Rowlandson reveals remarkably little of her life as a New England wife and mother; her narrative focuses almost exclusively on a three month period when her circle encompassed not home but wilderness, not Puritan society but "Heathen" hierarchies (2). This enforced dislocation from Puritan society and its expectations resulting from King Philip's War forces Rowlandson to refine her ideas of women's "proper" behavior. Because war serves, in the words of Czeslaw Milosz, to redefine what is "natural" in life, tasks that would be considered unnatural--unfeminine and outside the boundaries of proper social behavior--for women during times of peace can become not only "natural," but feminine and socially acceptable during a war (63)[3]. During this unsettling period, scripture is the thread binding the realities

---

[3]Vaughan and Clark apply the sociological term "initiation" in an interesting way. During initiation, people moving from one social position to another

of Rowlandson's present existence to the expectations of her past. It serves as her touchstone when "Stripped of affectionate relationships, social identity, and familiar surroundings, Rowlandson is forced to re-create herself" (Shrager Lang 21). As her life in the wilderness forces her not only to rely upon herself, but to *admit* that she does so, Rowlandson's scriptural quotations become more frequent and more fervent. Attempting to re-contain herself within the values of Puritan Christianity, Rowlandson relies on Biblical passages to illustrate precedences for her extreme experiences. Consciously or unconsciously, however, the scriptures that Rowlandson chooses to illustrate her Puritan humility instead exemplify her new-found self-sufficiency and strength. Allying herself with scriptural authorities, Rowlandson partakes of their power even as she claims to humble herself before their knowledge.

Thus, though Mary Rowlandson's captivity narrative is, one level, a pious account in which she claims again and again that reading the scriptures quiets her spirit and quells her desire to act in her own defense so that:

> Many times I should be ready to run out against the heathen, but
> the scripture would quiet me again, Amos 3:6 "Shall there be evil
> in the city and the Lord hath not done it. . . ." (58)

---

undergo three distinct phases: separation, margin, and reaggregation. Arguing that captives witness the majority of what is later written about during the marginal, or liminal, phase, Vaughan and Clark describe this time outside of Puritan society as inherently free from its social constraints: "Cut loose from his [the captive's] normal guideposts of language and social relationships, he entertained ideas and values that colonial New England did not allow. Old patterns were abandoned and new ones acquired" (12). This acquisition of new values must have been doubly freeing and terrifying for women, who had no experience of self-governance prior to their captivity. Just as minister and ex-captive John Williams could preach and moralize about his experiences after his release, he also brought to his time with the Indians practical and scholarly knowledge about the creation of social strictures. Rowlandson--and by extension the other women released by war from social constructs--brought to her captivity no such experience. In consequence, these women's feelings of inadequacy and transgression when they were forced to make their own value judgements must have been exponentially amplified, and their eventual loss of this freedom correspondingly more painful.

56

As it counsels her to "wait patiently upon the Lord," scripture also empowers Rowlandson to act in the manner of powerful men, thereby shattering the very Puritan society that it is meant to recreate.[4]

At one point, after waiting weeks for the militia to free her--and watching Indian children forge rivers that her deliverers found uncrossable--Rowlandson questions her "protected" status in Puritan society.[5] After she and her captors cross a river with a regiment close behind, Rowlandson remarks that the squaws carried their children across the river, yet as for the soldiers:

> this river put a stop to them. God did not give them the courage or the activity to go after us; we were not ready for so great a mercy as victory and deliverance (44).

Rowlandson's struggle to believe what she says is paramount here; devoutly believing that God's mercies are past human understanding; desirous of waiting "patiently upon the Lord;" attempting to shepherd a secular audience to the Lord, and yet burning with a slow anger at the human incompetence of the New England militia, Rowlandson cannot keep her discontent from seeping through the seams of her story. Earnest Christian though she is, Rowlandson's ultimate decree that her non-rescue is less the fault of the soldiers than the will of God rings false and highlights her uncomfortable position as both upholder and deconstructor of Puritan values.

Later, Rowlandson defiantly disagrees with the comment by her son (also

---

[4]While on one level all Christian women should partake of the power of scripture as they live their lives guided by it, Rowlandson's captivity narrows the gap between her life and the scriptures that she imitates. If she had not experienced the suffering of the prophets in the past--and thereby could not participate fully in their grace--her suffering *in the name of God* gives her leave to claim full communion with the Biblical prophets that she quotes.

[5]In varying degrees, the ideal of woman as "protected" by men (most especially from that most dangerous of pursuits, war) has informed the experiences of all American women. When their participation in war forces women to question the reality and desirability of this protected status, it also begins to break down its inherent social barriers.

a captive) that "he was as much grieved for his father as for himself" (54) with the cutting

> I wondered at his speech, for I thought I had enough upon my spirit in reference to myself to make me mindless of my husband and everyone else, they being safe among their friends. (54)

Here, though her son touts the Puritan party line, his comment does not cause Rowlandson shame, but rather "wonder." A Christian woman, raised to be mindful of the needs of others before her own, Rowlandson is confronted by a situation in which she must proclaim her own needs paramount: her husband and friends are safe, and she is a starving, grieving captive. In a moment unique in Puritan literature, Rowlandson declares herself the legitimate center of her own life and text; her conscious self-referentiality (*I* had enough upon *my* spirit with reference to *myself*) emphasizes and re-emphasizes that *she* is in command, *her* predicament is paramount, *she* is the only capable judge of her actions and their effect. Rowlandson's war-related position as other to Puritan society is what makes this radical declaration acceptable to her reader. She highlights how her captivity forces her to see things differently as she muses:

> *Now* I had time to examine all my ways. My conscience did not accuse me of unrighteousness toward one or other. . . . As David said, "Against thee, Thee only, have I sinned. . ." (56) (italics mine)

Rowlandson and David speak with one voice here; as David denigrates his auditor's ability to judge him, so too does Rowlandson strip from Puritan society its ability to censor her. In this way, Rowlandson's war experiences provide her with a consciousness of self in the singular rather than in the communal; as her relationship to God rather than to God's chosen becomes paramount, she makes it clear that she needs no human approval for experiences that God has ordained.[6]

---

[6]While it would appear that Rowlandson's focus on God and his judgement should coincide with Puritan Christianity, this was not the case. Puritan Christianity, as represented by its churches (of which Rowlandson's husband was

58

Because of this, as Rowlandson's "removes" take her further and further form Puritan society, her use of scripture becomes more direct and more empowering. With her third remove, Rowlandson begins to introduce her scripture with the curious disclaimer, "I may say as [David, Job, Paul, Hezekiah, the Psalmist, etc.]." After explaining how she was threatened by her captors with death if she stirred from her wigwam, Rowlandson continues, "Now I may say with *David, 2 SAM. xxiv. 14, I am in a great strait*" (49). That, because of her experiences, Rowlandson *may* say as these Biblical men "now" suggests that others may *not* do so. Rather than simply reading her bible for spiritual guidelines prior to her actions (as when she reminds herself to "wait upon the Lord:), Rowlandson also begins to quote the Bible as moral justification for actions she has already accomplished. At one point, Rowlandson tells how she steals food from a child and justifies her actions through scripture; telling of a particular search for food, Rowlandson continues:

> Then I went to another wigwam where there were two of the English children. The squaw was boiling horses' feet; then she cut me off a little piece and gave one of the English children a piece also. Being very hungry, I had quickly eat up mine, but he child could not bite it, it was tou[g]h and sinewy but lay sucking, gnawing chewing, and slabbering of it in the mouth and hand. Then I took it of the child and ate it myself and savory it was to my taste. Then I may say [as] Job, chap. 6:7, "The things that my soul refused to touch are as my sorrowful meat." Thus the Lord

---

a minister), argued that believers must act together to interpret God's will and to weed out undesirable (ungodly) actions. Rowlandson's declaration that only God can judge her actually mirrors the antinomian beliefs of Ann Hutchinson, or the even more extreme beliefs of Roger Williams who declared, at one point, that he could only worship alone as all other communion was tainted. That such a declaration was not only accepted by Rowlandson's audience, but considered a testimony of Church values, demonstrates the power of war to allow voice to those who were silenced in times of peace. Rowlandson can dismiss her society's ability to judge her because she writes of a time when her society is very notably absent; had Rowlandson written not about her captivity but about her time as wife and mother living within Puritan society, such a manifesto would have been egregiously unacceptable.

made refreshing what at another time would have been an abomination. (60)

That Rowlandson chooses to tell this story at all is surprising, given its unflattering portrait of her as a woman unrepentant for stealing food from a child: just as we expect her to say that she helped the child to chew the tough meat, she casually remarks that she ate it herself. Had the child been Indian (given the Colonial view of Natives as sub-human heathens), Rowlandson's lack of remorse for leaving it to starve would have seemed less unsettling. But the child is not Indian but English, and Rowlandson still unhesitatingly reveals how she "took [the food] of the child and ate it myself." As she moves geographically and emotionally farther and farther from the expectations of Puritan society, Rowlandson insists more stringently upon her value as an individual: I matter; I am hungry; I will eat. Her use of scripture reifies this declaration of self-worth; as long as she may insist as *Job* that things once inedible become edible in times of crisis, there is no room for her reader to question the moral correctness of her actions.[7] Scripture, in this instance, allows Rowlandson not only to tell of actions unimaginable within Puritan society (compare her earlier horror at the death of her sister's children and her own young daughter with her casual consignment of this child to starvation) but to justify and even to brag of them.

In this same manner, Rowlandson exclaims:

> O, the wonderful power of God that I have seen and the experiences that I have had! I have been in the midst of those roaring lions and savage bears that feared neither God nor man nor the devil, by night and day, alone and in company sleeping all sorts together, and yet not one of them ever offered me the least abuse of unchastity to me in word or action. Though some are

---

[7]Immediately after Rowlandson steals the food, she describes how her captors threaten to kill her if she begs again; her reply, that "they had as good knock [her] in the head as starve [her] to death" is an unapologetic nose-thumb at the power of her captors. Unprotected by the Colonists, she is also in some sense unthreatened by the Indians. *She will survive,* first and foremost, despite the vagaries of either power structure.

> ready to say I speak for my own credit, I speak it in their presence
> of God and to his glory. God's power is as great now and as
> sufficient to save as when he preserved Daniel in the lion's den or
> the three children in the fiery furnace. I may well say as his {sal
> 1-7:12, "Oh, give thanks unto the Lord for He is good, for His
> mercy endureth forever." Let the redeemed of the Lord say so
> whom He hath redeemed form the hand of the enemy, especially
> that I should come away in the midst of so many hundreds of
> enemies quietly and peaceably and not a dog moving his tongue.
> (70)

If the redeemed of the Lord may speak, Rowlandson argues, she who has been
not only spiritually but physically redeemed by God may speak "especially."
Again, scripture enables Rowlandson to proclaim both her own worth and that of
her tale; her insistence that she was not only redeemed from "the midst of so
many hundreds of enemies" but that this was done so "quietly and peaceably that
"not a dog [moved] his tongue" place her qualifications as speaker above even
that required by scripture. Thus, while Vaughan and Clark's argument that, "For
women, especially, the return to New England society posed problems of
readjustment and reacceptance," is certainly valid, the barriers to this
readjustment are not, as they suggest, related exclusively to the captives' need to
prove themselves unmolested sexually (14). Rowlandson does declare that she
was not "offered the least abuse of unchastity" during her sojourn, but this
remark seems formulaic and unimpassioned; the energy in this passage is in
Rowlandson's declaration that she may speak, not in her denial of abuse. The
problem for Rowlandson--a Puritan clergyman's wife--is that her experiences have
left her morally tainted if physically pure. Her narrative, then, cannot but give
voice to the thrill of freedom even as it record the degrading pain of captivity.
That the real-life speaker behind the voice may have remained unaware of this
speaks eloquently to the generativity inherent in authorship itself.

Scripture is not an empowering force, however, in the narrative of a
woman as told by a pillar of patriarchy. In Rowlandson's text, scripture
empowers the individual female voice. Scripture in the roughly contemporaneous
A Narrative of Hannah Dustan's Notable Deliverance From Captivity, however,

serves to help recontain a radical woman within Puritan society. If Rowlandson's tale is essentially one of waiting, Hannah Dustan's captivity narrative is a story of bloody resolve and victorious battle; in it, Dustan tells how she waited for her Indian captors to sleep before killing ten of them (not sparing children) in her fury at her capture. The historical figure of Dustan goes even further, calmly scalping her abductors and carrying her trophies to the Massachusetts General Assembly to claim a reward of fifty pounds.

Dustan's actions show her to be a woman capable of protecting herself and--perhaps even more troubling to Puritan philosophy--willing to avenge herself. Unlike Rowlandson, however, who tells her own story, Dustan exists only as the questionable "heroine" of Cotton Mather's captivity narrative. Not surprisingly, given Mather's double antecedents of spiritual autobiography and sermon, Hannah Dustan's story ostensibly is told in order to probe the existence of the ruling hand of God. However, "within the appropriate story. . .there are elements to suggest that God's agency might have been less clearly involved than Mather would have liked" (Davidson 88). That is, there are moments when the social order that Mather's God represents is strained unmercifully--most notably in Hannah Dustan's response to being made a prisoner of war.

It is significant that while Rowlandson turns to scripture to explain, justify, and contain her incredible experiences, Mather uses only one direct scriptural quotation throughout his text. Vaughan and Clark suggest that the decreasing use of scripture in later captivity narratives reflects a lessening of "Puritan piety and clerical influence," but this explanation is unsatisfactory when it is applied to the writing of Cotton Mather, a staunch advocate of Puritan ideals and a clergyman (24). Instead, I would suggest that the absence of direct scriptural quotations in Mather's text reflects a desire to recontain and circumscribe Dustan's actions; Rowlandson's narrative after all, is a case in point of the power granted to women when they ally themselves with scripture. Instead of using scripture to validate Dustan's *de facto* claim to self-sufficiency--indeed, instead of allowing Dustan to explain her own actions--Mather is the final interpreter and judge of Dustan's story. As he remarks, "I must now publish what these poor women assure me" (163). Unlike Rowlandson, who had the scriptural authority to "declare the works of the Lord," Mather reduces Dustan to a "poor woman" whose experiences he "must" explain by substituting scriptural interpretations for scripture itself.

Further, like Frederick Douglass, who needed three successive autobiographies before he could tell of a life lived so outside mainstream white society in its voice, so too did Cotton Mather require three refinements of Dustan's tale in order to deproblematize her actions. Having first published the narrative as an appendix to *Humiliations Followed with Deliverance* (Boston, 1697), Mather added an "improvement of the foregoing narrative" to its second incarnation before expanding Dustan's story even further in *Decennium Luctuosum* (Boston, 1699) and *Magnalia Christi Americana* (London, 1702). Clearly, the bare-bones chronicle of Dustan's war experience required extreme doctoring before it could be presented as an exemplar of Christian behavior.[8] Perhaps the most striking appearance of Mather's heavy-handed editing is evident in the rhetorical gymnastics he performs in an effort to relate the precise actions of a woman killing in her own defense. Records indicate that Dustan herself was in the congregation when Mather first preached his sermon based on her experiences. Hence (and because the General Assembly had awarded her fifty pounds for the scalps she presented them, thereby legitimizing and publicizing her tale), we can assume that Mather was forced to stick to the bare facts of Dustan's capture and escape. Mather, then, was left with what must have been an untenable situation--that of somehow encapsulating the incredibly powerful narrative of Hannah Dustan within a social and religious order that did not even permit women to speak in church when they came to make pleas for church membership. Thus, it must have been with full awareness of the gaping chasm

---

[8]According to Vaughan and Clark, "Presumably Hannah Dustan served many New Englanders as living example of Christian piety and courage" (6).

between the morality of Puritan norms and Dustan's actions that Mather began his sermon. And, short as the sermon is (Dustan's narrative occupies only three pages of Mather's sermon, while his telling of Hannah Swarton's captivity takes fourteen pages), Mather's rhetoric struggles continually to diffuse the power of her actions.

The narration of Dustan's capture and subsequent decision to escape is straightforward; directly preceding the killings, Mather tells us, "But on April 30, while they were yet it maybe about an hundred and fifty miles from the Indian town, a little before the break of day when the whole crew was in a dead sleep,"--and to this point, all proceeds smoothly. However, when Mather reaches the point in his narrative where he must detail Dustan's actions in killing and scalping her captors to free herself, his authorial tactics shift dramatically; it is only after six justifications that Mather hints at Dustan's actual vengeance. He reveals:

> But, on April 30, while they were yet it may be about an hundred and fifty miles from the Indian town, a little before break of day when the whole crew was in a dead sleep (Reader, see if it prove not so!) one of these women took up a resolution to imitate the actions Jael upon Sisera [Judges 4], and being where she had not her own life secured by any law unto her, she thought she was not forbidden by any law to take away the life of the murderers by whom her child had been butchered. She hardened the nurse and the youth to assist her in this enterprise, and they all furnishing themselves with hatchets for this purpose, they struck such home-blows upon the heads of their sleeping oppressors that ere they could any of them struggle into any effectual resistance at the feet of those poor prisoners, "They bowed, the fell, they lay down; at their feet they bowed, they fell where they bowed; there they fell down dead." [Judges, 5:27]

> Only one squaw escaped, sorely wounded, from them in the dark, and one boy whom they served asleep, intending to bring him away with them, [who] suddenly waked and scuttled away from this desolation. But cutting off the scalps of the ten wretches, they came off and received fifty pounds from the General Assembly of the province as a recompense of their action, beside which they received many presents of congratulation from their more private friends. (164)

Before Mather, in his text, gets to the killing he stops and inserts:

1) "(Reader, see if it prove not so!)"--a testimony to the proof of the forthcoming (and obviously highly incredible) narration;

2) "One of these women"--a pointed omission of Dustan's name, and a mute testimony that he is more comfortable with the woman whom he creates than he is with the actual woman who killed ten people;

3) "took up a resolution to imitate the actions of Jael upon Sisera [Judges 4]--a Biblical antecedent that puts religious law on the side of Dustan's actions, even while it makes her decisiveness a mere act of mimicry;

4) "and, being where she had not her own life secured by any law unto her,"--a pivotal declaration that asserts that Dustan acted as she did--and that these actions are acceptable--only because she was *outside* Puritan society at the time;

5) "she thought she was not forbidden by any law"--a second, fascinating reminder that Dustan acted outside of Puritan society that actually questions what is asserts, (and so sets no precedence for other women); since Dustan only *"thought"* that she was not forbidden by law, the possibility is left open that she is wrong in her assumption, and (eventually) can be chastised for her actions;

6) "to take away the life of the murderers by whom her child had been butchered."--a justification of her actions on the grounds of motherly love which demands revenge on the murderers of her child (who, we can assume, could be the murderers of other mothers' children if not dispatched).

As he continues, Mather steps gingerly around Dustan's primal violence, explaining the Dustan first "heartened" her fellow prisoners to help her, then that they all "furnished themselves with clubs," then that they struck blows on "the heads of their sleeping oppressors" so that none of them struggled or suffered. But then, instead of the final death of the Indians that we expect, Mather interjects the Biblical quotation, "They bowed, they fell, they lay down; at their feet they bowed, they fell where they bowed; there they fell down dead [Judges

5:27].[9] The next sentence that we read is "only one squaw escaped." And so the ultimate fact of the death of the Indians is circumvented; we are guided form a glimpse of a biblical death, to a vision of an actual survivor. Mather's sole direct scriptural quotation keeps the Indian dead form darkening the pages of Mather's tale, and so saves him from truly accounting for the blood on Dustan's hands.

While Rowlandson tries--and fails--to normalize her situation through the use of scripture, Mather uses scripture to deproblematize Dustan's radical departure form the norms of Puritan society. Try though she might to encapsulate herself within scripture, again and again Rowlandson bursts through her own neat packaging. The scripture that she quotes to remind herself to "wait patiently upon the Lord" instead--to Rowlandson's dismay, it would seem--calls into question the religious and social foundation of Puritan society itself.[10] Thus, while Rowlandson's story is of a woman whose actions remain bounded, in the main, by Puritan guidelines as she waits for help from others, her ultimate understanding of herself as a moral and spiritual arbiter deconstructs the order of her society.

Dustan's narrative, in contrast, is the story of a woman who assumes the very masculine power to protect and avenge herself. In this instance, war sanctifies Dustan's killing as her peacetime society does not. Her story, however, told (and "improved" upon) by the most famous advocate for maintaining the *status quo* of Puritan society, becomes an attempt to recontain a woman's known,

---

[9]Mather's choice of quotation here serves, once again, to strip the power from Dustan's actions. Rather than referring to a Biblical justification for killing, Mather records an oddly circular, passive sentence that focuses on the powerless acts of weeping, bowing, and falling down. Nowhere is his discomfort with the actual strength inherent in Dustan's resolve more apparent.

[10]This questioning of the society the spawned war (whether the author allies herself with one side of combatants or the other within the war) is yet another identifying feature of women's war narratives.

unsocial actions within the pale of Puritan social order. All of Mather's editing, however, cannot conceal the basic fact that Dustan kills in her own defense and then demands recognition for her deeds. Because of this, that Dustan does not tell her own story conceals less than we might expect; what we know of her actions (and her willingness to incur notoriety by demanding payment for the scalps that she takes) speaks eloquently to how her life is changed by war. Ironically, although Mather's abstemious use of scripture removes any vestige of Dustan's voice from the text--she speaks neither through her own words nor through those borrowed from the prophets. Mather's his studied attempts to strip the power from Dustan's actions reveal instead just how powerful a woman talking about war can be.

WORKS CITED

Andrews, William L, Sargent Bush, Jr., Annette Kolody, Amy Shrager Lang, and Daniel B. Shea. *Journeys in New Worlds: Early American Women's Narratives*. Wisconsin: University of Wisconsin Press, 1990.

Davidson, Phebe. *Religious Impulse in Selected Autobiographies of American Women (c. 1630-1893): Uses of the Spirit*. Lewiston: Edwin Mellen Press, Ltd., 1993.

Elshtain, Jean Bethke. *Women and War*. U.S.A.: Basic Books, Inc., 1987.

Milosz, Czeslaw. *The Captive Mind*. NY: Alfred A. Knopf, 1953.

Shea, Daniel B., Jr. *Spiritual Autobiography in Early America*. Princeton: Princeton University Press, 1968.

Vaughan, Alden T. and Edward W. Clark. *Puritans Among the Indians: Accounts of Captivity and Redemption 1676-1721*. Cambridge: Harvard University Press, 1981.

"Praying for an Earthquake": Personal Narrative as Colonial Conversion in "The Autobiography of Increase Mather"

Joanne M. Gaudio

University of Wyoming

Increase Mather belonged to the generation of New England Puritans whom Perry Miller described as bewildered, confused, and chagrined, but who, nevertheless, did not falter in their determination to bring their people back to the virtues of the Founders (Miller 15). Overall, "The Autobiography of Increase Mather" is a conversion narrative for New England in which Mather publicly relates his own and New England's experiences of sinfulness and repentance as he attempts to prove his subjects' worthiness as "visible saints." In doing so, he reveals the Puritans' true errand, "the union of saint and society" (Bercovitch 88), which he unknowingly helped to transform from a theological to a secular concept, forging "a ritual of progress" which propelled New England into the future (101). As part of this progress, the idea of God's absolute and inscrutable authority evolved into the more hopeful idea that man, by his own efforts, could influence God's actions (White 37). Increase Mather did not consciously give up his belief in the superiority of the Founders, since he often looked into himself to see if he measured up. Without realizing it, however he also looked forward to a new future which he helped to define.

Mather wrote his autobiography in three sections. Part One[1] is a traditional spiritual narrative written in 1685 when Mather was at the height of his powers. Mather wrote Part Two in 1694, and it primarily concerns his mission for Massachusetts in England at the time of the Charter Crisis. Part Three, written between 1696 and 1715, both ties up loose ends and provides the opportunity for a nostalgic review of the past (AB 272-274). Together the three parts reveal both the devout minister and the image of a covenanted community Increase Mather wanted the world to remember, and the shrewd politician and the divisive colony that Mather and New England became. Since it is beyond the scope of this essay to consider all the theological political and cultural ramifications of the "Autobiography," I will limit my discussion to the specific instances where Mather's concept of authority shifts. As his rhetoric reflects, he implicitly grows to rely more on himself and unconsciously moves toward assuming some of God's authority, thus influencing his own and New England's fate.

Daniel Shea maintains that spiritual autobiographers talk to "their posterity, to their countrymen, to God, and to themselves" (xxviii). Mather's designated audience was his "dear children," for whom he hopes his words "might be a means to cause you to give yourselves entirely to the Lord Jesus, and to endeavor to walk with God" (AB 277). Near the end of the manuscript he shows that he also addressed succeeding generations, when on his seventieth birthday he asks God to "bless my Family and children and childrens children after I am gone from them" (355). In both cases he offers himself as an example of a visible saint for the instruction of his immediate family and his descendants. He also wrote for himself, to recall the ways in which God had favored him, and for God, to "prove" that he had been a good Puritan. In addition, Mather reveals

---

[1]The part designations are based on Editor Michael G Hall's introduction to "The Autobiography of Increase Mather" (AB 272-74). Citations to the "Autobiography" are designated by AB.

another audience, although not one he expected to read his words, as, in 1684, he begins praying for the people collectively as "New England."

Mather begins Part One by recording his birth "at dorchester in New England June 21. in the year 1639" and validating his membership in the "elect": "My father was a faithfull and eminent minister of Christ, [and]. . .[m]y mother was a very Holy praying woman" who on her death bed begged her youngest son to enter the ministry (AB 277-8). He then describes his conversion at age fifteen, his graduation from Harvard, and the beginning of his ministry in 1657 when he preached one of his first sermons "at dorchester" (279-80). Increase's son Cotton reports that his father preached this early sermon "in his Fathers Pulpit," and that Richard Mather "could scarce Pronounce the Blessing for the Tears" of pride and joy he shed[2] (*Parentator* 92). The impersonality of Increase's own account reveals his unconscious competition with his father at the same time as he embarked on a career of extolling the superiority of the Founders, of whom his father was a member, and thus displays one of the contradictions within Increase Mather that helped drive him into the future. Consciously he insisted on restoring the Founders' ways; unconsciously, in striving to surpass the Founders, he pushed himself and New England forward by extracting "the larger, vaguer, and more flexible forms of metaphor and myth" from the past and transforming them through the "ritual of progress" into the "new" New England (Bercovitch 101).

Mather left New England in 1657 to join his oldest brother in Dublin and take an M.A. at Trinity College (AB 281). He then preached in England until the Restoration, when he was "persecuted out of two places. . .before I was 22 years of age" (285). Unwilling to "conform and read the Common prayer," he returned to Boston in 1661, married, and finally settled there because, he says, "I apprehended that I might probably do more Service in my generation for Christ

---

[2]Cotton Mather reveals a number of things in *Parentator* (1724) that his father omits from the "Autobiography," including the disagreement between Richard and Increase Mather over the half-way covenant, and Increase's persecution of the Quakers.

and for his people, by settling in Boston, than in any other place where I was desired" (286-87). This need to serve was one of the driving forces of Mather's life.

In Boston, Mather at first resisted formal acceptance of the Teacher's position at Boston's North (Second) Church, but after several years he agreed, since "the Inhabitants as well as the church did by writing and subscribing their names signify their desires for my Continuance amongst them (AB 287). This was the first indication that Mather saw his mission as being to all New England; "inhabitants" referred to non-church residents of the community (Miller 150), who were required by law to attend and support the church (White 55), while "church" signified church embers. Yet at the same time, he "had also a great desire to return to England if liberty for Nonconformity should there be granted" (AB 287), a desire which may have been motivated by the stress of a public disagreement with his father over the half-way covenant."[3] Throughout his life, mather's longing to return to England waxed and waned in direct proportion to his degree of satisfaction with life in Massachusetts.

At this point, the "Autobiography" ignores the half-way covenant controversy, "[t]he great disagreement that. . .divided New England Puritans into two camps at mid-century" (Hall 55). At the Synod of 1662 Mather opposed the pro-baptism group led by his father and his Harvard tutor, Jonathan Mitchell. Instead of discussing the controversy, however, Mather records that after his ordination in 1664, at which his father assisted, he "was grievously molested with Temptations to Atheisme, whereby my spirit was much afflicted and broken" (287). Since Atheism may be defined a "[d]isregard of duty of God" (*OED*), Mather's "Atheisme" may have reflected his emotional distress at breaking the

---

[3]The majority view at the Synod of 1662 favored relaxation for the rules for the baptism of the children of baptized but unconverted second-generation Puritans. The minority objected that this would lead to further erosion of church principles (Hall 55-60).

fifth commandment to honor his father.[4] Ironically, the laity agreed with Increase Mather and did not at that time support the Synod's decision to accept the innovation in baptism. This led, in turn, to Mather's becoming a leader of the laity (Hall 60), a position which became crucial to New England at the time of the Charter Crisis. Concluding his account of those Temptations. . . .Hee is a rewarder of them that diligently seeke him" (AB 287), an early indication of his unconscious belief that God could be influenced to act (White 58).

After skipping the five years of disagreement with his father, Mather records Richard's death in 1669, followed by the death of his brother Eleazer three months later (AB 287). These deaths left him ill and depressed, and although his physical health returned "[b]efore the year 1670 was expired" (288), he suffered from bouts of depression for several more years. In 1670 he complained of "ephialtes" or nightmares which troubled him so much that he feared the onset of mania. He prayed and found temporary relief during a visit to the mineral springs at Lynn, where he reminded God that he should be cured "because I desire Health for the Lords sake and not for my owne, viz. that I might so service for God and for Christ" (291). The substance of this statement, that God should answer Mather's prayers because to do otherwise would not be in God's best interests, reflects what Eugene White calls a reduction in "the inscrutability, the implacability, and the uncontrollable exercise of God's power" (73). White points out that the second generation of Puritans moved toward the idea that "man was not totally impotent" before God's absolute authority but rather "possessed within himself substantial means to further his own salvation" (37). This was a natural extension of covenant theology which, through its

---

[4]In *Parentator* (1724) Cotton Mather records that at the Synod of 1662 Increase had "the Infelicity. . .to dissent from his own venerable father [Richard]. However such was the Wisdom and Goodness on both sides, that there was no Diminution of their Delight in one another." (112). If Increase suffered, he kept it inside, and it is not unlikely that the pain would emerge in "Temptations to Atheisme" and a desire to return to England (AB 287).

emphasis on God's mercy and willingness to enter a covenant with man, "encouraged a posture which tended to magnify man's efforts and to minimize the doctrine of election" (42). Thus, Increase Mather's own words reflect a changing theology, even though publicly he continued to support conservative Puritan principles, as when in 1692 he encouraged disputation of "Armnianisme," the idea the man had some power to affect his own grace (AB 344-45).

Mather's depression was partially mitigated by publication of his first book, *The Mystery of Israel's Salvation* (1669), and of his father's biography, *The Life and Death of Richard Mather* (1670). Before writing the biography, he listed "[t]he threefold wish of the chief of sinners": to do something special for God, to leave some good behind him after he was dead, and to "suffer and dy for the sake of my dear God" after his work was done (AB 288-89). Two months later he prayed again for these "wishes of my soul," and he gave reasons why God would "Answer my poor prayers," among them, "1. Because I drew nigh to him, therefore his blessings will draw night to me. 2. Because the things which I asked, and the end why I asked them was for Gods glory. Not for my owne sake, but for Gods sake" (290). Mather's wish to serve was often accompanied by the idea that God would do well by him because he was working for God. This again suggests his unconscious acceptance of the idea that what he did would have an influence on his salvation.

In *The Life and Death of Richard Mather*, Increase records his father's deathbed appeal for support of the Fifth Proposition (the half-way covenant) (58), although he neither discusses the controversy nor reveals his own reversal of opinion on the issue which followed his father's death. Another reason for excluding the controversy from his father's biography, in addition to Mather's personal pain, may have been his need to keep his presentation of Puritan unity and purpose pure for succeeding generations. In his portrayal of Richard Mather, Increase personified the myth of the founders and their errand, drawing a picture of a successful union of saint and society.

In 1673 Increase Mather delivered "a publick solemn warning of judgment near at hand. . . .*The day of Trouble is near."* As he writes, "It was much in my thoughts that God would visit with the sword. . . .Afterwards I saw that those thoughts were from God. For in the year of 1675 the warr with the Indians (which lasted for several years) began" (AB 301-02). *The Day of Trouble* was one of the great jeremiads, delivered not just to Mather's congregation but to the entire population of New England (Stout 75). In enlisting all of New England, saints and sinners, in the fight against sin, Mather moved away from the Founders' perception of New England as simply a convenient place to preserve the "Kingdom of Light" (Middlekauff 33) and toward the idea that New England itself, the embodiment of visible sainthood, was what mattered.

"The interest of New-England was Religion, which did distinguish us from other English Plantations," Mather writes in *The Day of Trouble* (1674), "but now we begin to espouse a Worldly Interest" (22-23). "[T]herefore," he continues, "we may conclude that he [God] will scourge us for our backsliding" (26). However, he ends with the hope that "if we humble our selves deeply and unfeignedly, God cannot finde in his heart to destroy us" (28). This final suggestion that salvation was still possible was common to the second-generation jeremiads, which "set out to transform threat into promise" (Bercovitch 95). What Mather was telling New England was that by working hard to reach the goal of the errand--to merge all the people into one reformed whole--they could achieve fulfillment of the covenant. This gave the people direction and purpose in their lives while New England worked its way toward the future (95). It also furthered the idea the God would react to man's actions, reinforcing the lessening of God's inscrutable authority (White 50).

The jeremiads developed because as New England's population grew and diversified, the people changed in ways which the clergy misconstrued as social and spiritual decline. In response, the clergy claimed "[s]pecial powers of prediction" not seen before in New England. Attempting to bolster their declining status, "ministers emphasized their superior prophetic powers in strong words intended to set them apart form the pious rank and file" (Stout 77). The result was prophecy as heard in *The Day of Trouble*, a risky business since the "ministers preached themselves into a corner. . . .[and] [f]or their own credibility and legitimacy, they needed a disaster even more than they needed" the people to reform (77). King Philip's War, Mather's "warr with the Indians," provided the necessary disaster.

Mather donned the mantle of prophet again when "[d]uring the warr Time, observing the murmurings of the people,. . .I was verily perswaded that God would punish that iniquity with some mortal disease, and accordingly did I in publick 3 times declare as much" (AB 302). Some people objected to this life-threatening prophecy, but epidemics of "mortal feavors . . . and the small pox. . .whereby many dyed" proved the prophet accurate. As a result, Mather notes, "the divine providence put into my hands special advantage for service amongst his people" (302). This service was his ability to influence the General Court to pass "several wholesome laws for the suppressing of sin" (302)[5]. Thus, his public success in predicting God's actions enhanced his prestige as a servant of New England.

In 1676 Mather once again assumed the role of prophet, writing that "I was strongly possessed with fears that Boston would be punished with that judgment of Fire" (AB 302), not an uncommon occurrence in a town build predominantly of wood. Mather twice preached sermons resulting from his fear, and the day after the second sermon, a fire broke out in Boston which consumed his home, his church, and "several other dwellings" (303). However, he found divine providence at work amidst the ashes, for "God remembered mercy in this judgment. . . .And within two years God gave me a far better house. And now for the space of halfe a year I preached at other meetinghouses in Boston" (303). This fulfilled prophecy too, added to his influence in the wider community by showing that Increase Mather could "read" God, rendering Him less inscrutable.

---

[5]"Provoking Evils" (1675), *Several Laws and Orders Made at the Sessions of the General Court* (Hall 110).

William C. Spengemann and L.R. Lundquist suggest that as a person writes his life, he may assume the character of the prophet, one "who interpret[s] the complex relationship between present and future" (504) and aims "to define the mythic significance of daily activity" (506). As a Puritan minister in mid-seventeenth-century New England, Increase Mather strove to maintain his hold over the people for their own good, and in doing so, he adopted the prophet's role (Stout 81). In addition he revealed his success as a prophet to his descendants as he reinforced their faith in divine providence and the power of God and showed his special relationship with God. He did not realize that in doing the latter, he was also implicitly lessening God's authority in favor of his own.

To the Puritan clergy, prophesying meant "the interpretation and expounding of Scripture and the preaching of the Gospel" (*OED*). Yet at this time in New England, Increase Mather and other ministers, attempting to hold on to their authority, carried their role of prophesying a step further and claimed to have received God's word directly. In *The Day of Trouble* the prophecy was generalized and given a scriptural basis. When Mather later predicted the smallpox epidemic and the fire, the prophecy became more specific but the scriptural basis was still generalized. However, the day before the fire destroyed his meetinghouse, Mather preached on "Rev. 3.3. 'Remember how you hast received and heard'" (AB 303). The full text includes God's warning that He can strike at any time, but the fragment Mather quotes seems to claim fame for the prophet. Mather did not see that in his acts of predictive prophecy he assumed the mantle of direct spokesman for God in a way quite different from the clergy's earlier role.

In 1679, a Synod was convened "to enquire into the causes of God's displeasure against New England and scripture expedients for Reformation" (AB 305). Mather wrote the Synod result as well as the Preface to the Confession of Faith (1680) the following year (305). "The Synod's Work," published as *The Necessity for Reformation* (1679), resembled *The Day of Trouble*. It urged the people to reform and instructed the state that "[i]f therefore People be unwilling to doe what justice and reason calls for, the magistrate is to see them doe their duty in this matter" (*Synod's Work* 434). This encouragement of the state to adopt a God-like role in chastising people reluctant to reform was another example of the changing idea of the covenant. While the seventeenth-century Massachusetts magistracy had always acted in cooperation with the churches, this direction to the Magistrates "to see them [the people] doe their duty in this matter" (434) sounded more like God's job of chastising sinners. In addition, the ritual of covenant renewal which the Synod urged on the churches (435) was also a sign of the changing times since its primary aim was to pressure the half-way church members to complete their membership. This was a long way from the original Puritan idea that people should worship God with no thought for their own salvation (White 58).

This first part of the "Autobiography" takes a political turn when Mather begins his discussion of the Charter Crisis: "In the latter end of this year, that came to pass, which occasioned no small Trouble and Temptation to me" (AB 307). The trouble was both political and personal; the temptation may have been to see himself as the savior of New England, again assuming some of God's authority. The Charter Crisis changed New England from a self-governing Puritan theocracy to a secular royal colony. In 1676, Edward Randolph traveled to Boston to investigate the colony's affairs on behalf of the Committee for Trade and Plantations. When he returned to England, his report influenced the government to demand either changes in or revocation of the Massachusetts charter (Hall 188). Increase Mather supported those who resisted change, believing that the theocracy, which the old charter made possible, was necessary to keep the covenant (Stout 119).

When England demanded in 1683 that Massachusetts submit to changes in their charter, Mather was asked for his opinion. The resulting pamphlet,

"Arguments against relinquishing the Charter," [6] states clearly that Massachusetts had no right to give up "the inheritance of your fathers. . . .without the consent of the body of the people" (Arguments" 79). Again Mather helped to foster the changing view of New England. At the same time he supported the theocracy, he pushed the idea that New England must maintain its "auncient rights and priviledges" (AB 333). The end of the "Arguments" explains how Mather could now intermix the roles of minister and politician: "There is a sixth commandment. Men may not destroy their political any more than their natural lives. . . .The civil liberties of the people of New England are part of the inheritance of their father; and shall they give that inheritance away? (81).

This was both a refusal to accept appeasement and a justification for mather's later acceptance of the new charter which saved the colony's political life and permitted continuation of the Errand in changed form.

The following January, Boston's freemen met "to consider what they should do," and when Mather was invited to speak at the meeting he told them, "wee shall sin against God if wee vote an Affirmative to it.'" He related the biblical story of Naboth, who, when Ahab demanded his vineyard, said, "God forbid that I should give away the Inheritance of my Fathers'" (AB 308). Mather concluded by urging the freemen to refuse submission, for "if wee do it not, we keep ourselves still in the hand of God. . .and who knoweth what God may do for us?" (308). As he told the freemen, "I have discharged my conscience in

---

[6]Murdock thinks that the "Arguments," found in the Hutchinson Papers, may be Mather's statement (Murdock 153n. 107) Hall believes that they are not because they do not sound similar to any of Mather's other writing on the subject (384n. 18). Mather himself states:

> Several papers were brought to me. . .which argued for the negative. I put those arguments into Form, and added some more of my owne, and then communicated them to some of the Magistrates. . . .The other party conjectured me to be the author of the M.ss. and were not a little displeased thereat. Nevertheless I believe it was a good worke, and I hope acceptable to the Lord. (AB 307-08)

thus delivering myself to you'" (308), and by "you" he meant New England, the entire people, saints and sinners alike (Middlekauff 99-100).

Six months later Mather discovered the price for his outspokenness. A letter he sent to Amsterdam expressing "the evill of the Times was interrupted and it proved "very easy for ill-minded men to wrest my words, and put their owne construction on them, so that my danger was very great" (AB 309). The result was then presented in London as coming from Increase Mather. Mather found some good in the experience because New England prayed for his deliverance from persecution. However, he quickly undermined his trust in divine providence with the vow:

> 'If God will save me from the evill designed against me, and if hee will be so gracious as to send tidings from London that hee has delivered me from the malice of those that have sought my soul, Then God shall be my God, and I will (Christ helping me) endeavor to do more for his glory than ever yet I have done.' (309)

This "if. . .then" construction sounds suspiciously like bargaining with God and shows again that even Increase Mather was influenced more than he realized by the changing concept of the covenant.

Mather next recalls the troubles facing him in August 1684, and in a list of his "Humble requests unto God in Jesus Christ," for the first time he specifically includes the request that God should "[b]e mindfull of his people every where, especially in New England" (AB 311). Again, in February of 1684/5, he includes "Save New England" in a list of "Humble Requests" (312). As the charter crisis heated up, the idea of New England as an entire people to be saved intensified. It also became apparent that Mather saw himself as one who would be instrumental in the work. "I was pleading with God for New England," he records (312), and describes how, after a period of prayer and fasting, he emerged form his study crying "God will deliver New England" over and over (313). Clearly he had again assumed the role of prophet, saying "[t]hose things I think were from the spirit of God" (313).

Part One of the "Autobiography" ends twice, highlighting Mather's multiple roles as minister, public servant, and father. The first time, news of the death of King Charles II answered Mather's prayers for the deliverance of New England, and his appointment as President Pro Tem of Harvard answered his need to serve. "Thus have I related the story of my owne life for more than 46 years, so farr as I am able to recollect, and think convenient to express," he says (AB 313-14). For the sake of convenience, he left out large chunks of both personal and New England history, but he conveyed the image of the man he wished his descendants to remember: a proud, scholarly, yet spiritually humble man of God who feared for the people of New England, but who believed that they could still return to the ways of their fathers and so divert God's wrath. Yet, unknown to himself, though his text he also drew the picture of a man who was changing with the times even as he clung to the past.

Part One ends again after a series of paragraphs about Mather's children and several diary entries expressing his spiritual state at different times. This ending underlines Mather's paternal role both within his own family and toward all of New England. He gives thanks for the opportunities God has given him to do service yet is "ashamed to think how little I have done for God" (AB 318), and he concludes with several scripture references which can also be read as referring to the coming difficulties for God's people. By December 24, 1685, the date of the last entry, Mather knew that New England was in for a fight over the charter, the basis of the theocracy. He had personally felt the malice of New England's opponents, the political situation was tense, and he may have anticipated his role in the coming struggle.

Mather's mission as an agent for Massachusetts in England dominates Part Two of the "Autobiography." He begins by mentioning three publications: *A Brief Discourse Concerning the Unlawfulness of Common Prayer Worship* (1686), *A Testimony Against several Prophane and Superstitious Customs* (1687), and *An Arrow Against Profane and Promiscuous Dancing* (1685). *A Testimony* was aimed at the new Royal government headed by Sir Edmond Andros, who arrived in late 1686, after the charter's final revocation, and who quickly antagonized the colony (Hall 206-07). The 1685 *Arrow* took a local dancing school to task, but it also denounced a popular English court pastime. After a brief discussion of these works, which he "looked upon. . .as my duty" (AB 319), Mather returns to overtly political considerations of the Charter Crisis.

In an attempt to stabilize his power base, James II granted a Declaration of Indulgence purporting to guarantee freedom of religion (Hall 207). Upon hearing the news in May 1687, Mather writes "I am now wayting and praying for an earthquake, which shall issue in the downfall of the Lords enemies and the exaltation of Christs Kingdome and Interest (AB 320). However, in spite of his expressed reliance on divine providence, he also took matters into his own hands and proposed that the ministers of New England should send an address of thanks to the King for his "declaration for liberty to Non-Conformists" (320). Mather then arranged for "some Gentlemen in London" to present the address to the King and reported that it was well received. Soon Mather "moved that our churches (and not the ministers only) might Thank the King for his declaration" (320). He agreed to deliver this message personally, and indicative of his increasing political stature, "My purpose for England was no sooner noysed abroad" than Randolph arranged for his arrest for "a pretended defamation," Mather's assertion that Randolph had engineered the forged letter episode. However, Mather relates that "the whole Jury cleared me. . . .Thus has God bin my Helper!" (321). Once again, divine providence served the entire people of New England by releasing Increase Mather from jeopardy.

"Observables dè my voyage to England in the year 1688" heads the main section of Part Two (AB 322). Ironically for the man who had suffered from a rivalry with his father, Mather left New England in much the same way his father had left Old England: disguised and fleeing arrest (*Life and Death* 52-3; AB 322-23). Whether he felt a sense of reenacting the original Great Migration is not apparent, but he was embarked on a mission back to his origins to save the charter which made New England possible. As he saw it at that time, if

Randolph and his adherents had their way, the errand would lose its meaning and the Puritans would lose their identity as God's chosen people. That Mather was able to change his thinking later and accept a new charter, realizing that the errand could transcend the government and survive, was a measure of the man and his percipience.

Quickly identifying himself as both political and religious representative of all New England's people, Mather tells how God's hand guided his journey: "The enemies of the good people in New England (who were in peculiar manner my enemies) failed in their designs of preventing my purpose for England" (AB 322). He describes how he eluded arrest and reached his ship, how God's providence saved them from dangers during the voyage, and how his own quick wits saved them from piratical fisherman off the coast of Cornwall. Finally he and his son Samuel disembarked at Weymouth, the town from which he had left England in 1661 (AB 324).

In this section, Mather mixes politics, divine providence, and self-justification. He describes his efforts to have the old charter restored, talks about the important men and women he met who encouraged and helped him, and shows how divine providence assures his success. He gained access to the Court as well as to many of England's noted statesmen. In addition, he writes, "my being brought into acquaintance with several of the Bishops proved advantageous to New England" (AB 327). As he works for New England's interests, he continues to emphasize the dual nature of New England that makes his own dual role possible: the "sacredness in the charter of New England" is due to the fact that "the charter of New England was a contract between the King and the first patentees" (327). The Founders, he points out, fulfilled their part of the contract by expanding the King's dominions; now it was up to the King to see that New England's charter privileges were continued (327). King James left England within the year, but Mather continued his appeals to the new Protestant King. William proved sympathetic and also a formidable bargainer.

Increase Mather and divine providence shared the credit for saving New

England's cause in 1689. Mather and Samuel booked passage home because charter restoration appeared assured. Bad weather delayed their sailing, however, and Samuel contracted smallpox, necessitating a return to London where Mather's friends assured him that God must have had a reason for the delay. The reason became apparent when, in the spring of 1690, Andros, Randolph, and two additional Massachusetts agents arrived and difficulties arose with New England's charges against Andros (AB 339-40). Since none of the agents, on the advice of their lawyer, would sign the charges, lest they be held personally responsible if Andros were acquitted (Hall 233), the committee investigating the matter not only dismissed the charges but also recommended returning Andros to New England as governor. Mather tirelessly lobbied supporters and refuting countercharges raised by Randolph and Andros, saying, "This people [New England] would have had a better Governor and Counsellors, nor any other priviledges, than what those places [the other colonies] have had not the providence of God prevented my Returning to them in 1689" (AB 341), and his detailed description of his work indicated his wish to share credit for the success with God.

While he was in England, Mather often prayed "that liberty, and prosperity, and a good Government might be restored to New England," and on one day he felt sure the "[m]y God, and the God of New England has heard prayer and delivered that his people. I know that it is so" (AB 341). Yet again, this was a long way from the original idea that people should worship God with no thought for their own salvation. It was, in fact, the new idea that if people worked hard for their faith, both they and society would be rewarded (White 58). Mather's thinking had evolved along with New England's theology, and he was teaching his descendants more than he knew.

Unfortunately for New England, the bill to restore the old charter died when Parliament was prorogued in January 1689/90. In the ensuing election the unsympathetic Tories gained the majority and killed any hope of reviving the old charter. As a result, Mather switched his lobbying activities to the Court and

King William. In the "Autobiography," Mather never states directly that he has accepted a new charter for New England. Instead, he relates a conversation with the King in which he thanks William for restoring "English liberties" and granting "some peculiar priviledges," one of which was permission to nominate the first royal governor (AB 336). Mather points out that this concession was due to his own influence with the King (336), leaving his descendants in no doubt about whom to thank for their present liberties.

At the end of his stay in England, Mather refers his readers to *A Brief Account Concerning Several of the Agents of New England* (1691), in which he insisted that losing the old charter was God's will. The new charter, he says, contains "all the Old, with the New, and more Ample privileges" (276), but he never refers directly to the major differences for the theocracy, the extension of the franchise to freeholders, which ended church control of the state (Hall 249), and the application of the doctrine of tolerance, which ended Puritan domination (Murdock 248). As with the half-way covenant controversy, Mather preferred to sidestep a controversial issue.[7] This was both politically shrewd, distancing him from the criticism he anticipated, and self-protective, thrusting responsibility back to God. Near the end of *A Brief Account*, Mather sums up his position and again revealed the contradictions within himself:

> However it shall be, whether my Counsels be followed or not, or whether my sincere Intentions, and unwearied Endeavors to serve New-England, find Acceptance with them or no, I have this to comfort my self with, That God has been so gracious to me, as to make me instrumental in obtaining for my Country a MAGNA CHARTA, whereby Religion and English Liberties, with some

---

[7]Mather was caught between the Tories, who castigated his chosen governor, and the Whig supporters of the old charter (Hall 264-71). However, although Mather's political stature waned in the aftermath of changing reality, he acted in accord with prevailing sentiment in New England (Hall 251-52). In addition, he put the onus for success or failure under the new charter squarely on the peoples' shoulders. If the people chose their elected assembly wisely, Mather said, "Religion will flourish: And if. . .not. . ., the fault will not be the New-Charter, but in themselves" (*Brief Account* 289).

> peculiar Priviledges, Liberties, and all Mens Properties, are
> Confirmed and Secured, (Allowance being given for the Instability
> of all Human Affairs) to Them and their Posterity for evermore.
> (296)

Once again, Mather took credit for the new charter and its benefits. This was
Mather the hero speaking, telling his descendants and all New England's people
that he "has taken the journey prescribed by the myth; and he looks back with
some satisfaction on events which seem to have fulfilled his initial expectations"
(Spengemann and Lundquist 509). He did not revive the old charter, his first
hope, but he secured the continuance of New England, and that, as he had come
to realize, was most important.

It was also Mather the prophet speaking. Although he did not realize it,
"[t]he Puritan commonwealth dreamed of and put in place by John Winthrop was
no more; the constitutional framework for the pluralistic, secular society that
would be inherited by John Adams was now in place" (Hall 251). However,
contrary to the fears of many, New England learned that it did not need the
theocracy to keep the church covenant. The people kept it voluntarily, and "New
England's mission would continue even though the Puritan state did not" (Stout
119). Mather must have sensed this possibility when he accepted and then
defended the new charter or he would not have endorsed it so readily. His
parenthetical, "(Allowance being given for the Instability of all Humane Affairs),"
showed his good grasp of political reality (*Brief Account* 296).

On his return to New England in 1691, Mather

> found the Countrey in a sad condition by reason of witchcrafts and
> possessed persons. . . .I therefore published my Cases of
> Conscience dè Witchcrafts etc--by which (it is sayd) many were
> enlightned, Juries convinced, and the shedding of more Innocent
> blood prevented." (AB 344)

He refers to the publication of *Cases of Conscience Concerning Evil Spirits*
(1692), which helped bring the witch hysteria to an end, but as with his previous
reticences about controversies in his life, he makes no mention of his son
Cotton's role in the situation.

"God has favored me with great opportunities to do service for his Name since my return to New England," Mather writes about his appointment as President of Harvard in 1692 (AB 344). Then, "I suppose I should not have had a thought about Returning to England again," but he did because "[s]ome things have hapned which do astonish me" (345). He does not explain that his work over the charter seemed to be repudiated when the old charter faction temporarily gained political ascendancy (Murdock 315-16), but he does say "that some workings of his [God's] providence seemed to Intimate that I must be returned to England again" (345). He is careful to add that God should only let him go if he could do more for God in England than at home, but it is clear that he was trying hard to influence God's decision. Mather ends Part Two feeling discouraged over "the Ingratitude of the people in New England (of which I have had experience)" and yet apparently satisfied that "[m]y opportunities in New England are great and singular. . . .And I have respect and honor enough" (347). All he really wanted was the chance to "glorify God and Jesus Christ, and do service to his dear people! Here I am, let God do with me what seemeth good in his sight" (347). At the end, he returned to his spiritual roots in an attempt to show his descendants that no matter how much New England had changed, submission to God's will was still at the center.

By the time he wrote the third part of the "Autobiography," Mather's political power had waned, and his concerns were primarily personal. He still yearned to return to England and constantly anticipated an answer to his prayers. When he suffered lameness, he searched for "the cause of this Rebuke" (AB 350). He was not unwilling to serve and he had not "bin negligent in studyes that this evil is come upon me. . . .Is it to rebuke me for my being willing to Return to England there to glorify the Name of Christ? (350). No, he decided, for his motive was pure; he wanted to return to England "to do greater service for Christ, than in New England I am capable of" (350). This was far from the submission to God's will which ended Part Two, even though he claimed that he was leaving the matter "wholly with God" (350).

He longed to return to England where he had felt successful and appreciated, and he could not understand why God was so slow in making it happen. An affirmative answer to his prayers would also have been a sign in these personally troubled times that God still favored him.

These years presented many irritants to Mather. Caught in a political bind, he resigned the Harvard presidency in 1701. He showed no Christian charity, however, in his spiteful report that "[t]hus pittifully did mr Willard [the new president] succeed. Hee managed the Commencement there in 1702, but so to expose himselfe to contempt and the Colledge to disgrace" (AB 351). In his anger, he compares himself to Christ, who "was ill rewarded by those whom He had layd under Infinite obligations of gratitude" (AB 351), and his frustration surfaces in the advice he leaves for his children--and New England's people:

> Doubtless, there is not a government in the world that has bin layd under greater obligations by a particular man than the Government here has bin by me. Nevertheless, I have received more discouragement in the work of the Lord by those in Government, than by all the men in the world besides. Let not my children put too much confidence in men. It may be such as they have layd under the greatest obligations of gratitude, will prove most unkind to them. I have often had experience of it (351-52).

By maintaining that all his work had been done in God's name, Mather equated the Government with those who rejected Christ and so found some consolation in the thought that he was suffering as Christ had. He also separated "those in Government" form "all the men in the world besides (351-52), keeping a firm grip on the importance of unity for New England's people.

In 1703 Mather showed no sign that he was content to leave the decision about the successor to his pulpit in God's hands. He did not want one of the new young ministers who "are too generally not so well affected to the Platform of church discipline as were to be desired. Also, they have a lazy way of reading all their sermons" (AB 353). The burden of living up to the past had shifted, and now it was the youngsters who threatened the covenant, especially those who espoused further relaxation of the rules for church membership and admitted almost anyone to full communion (Stout 122). However, once again, he never mentioned his own controversy--this time with Solomon Stoddard on the same subject.

In January 1708/9, not for the first time, Mather predicted his imminent death: "Oh, blessed be God if it be so!" (AB 353). He begged God's forgiveness for his sins and planned "to spend the few days I have to live in the world, in preaching on such subjects as I shall judge will be most for the good of souls" (354). He did not die in 1709, but he showed the distance he had come in twenty-five years in usurping some of God's absolute authority. In 1684 he had prayed for "[g]uidance as to what subjects to handle in my publick ministry" (311). In 1709 he deemed himself capable of judging what he should preach "for the good of souls" (354).

In a nostalgic and mellow mood after publication of a new book in 1711, Mather reflects: "If ever there was man in the world that had cause to be thankfull, I am Hee. . . .Bless the Lord O my Soul, and forget not all his benefits" (AB 358). He must have repeated this last phrase often to remind himself to be grateful to God because by late 1711 he was again worried about his successor at his church. Finally he recommended Joseph Sewall to take his place rather than another, unnamed young minister whose behavior "makes me fear that his heart is not right in the sight of God" (358). Again, Mather gives no indication of a willingness to leave the matter in God's hands.

A controversy over the location of a new meetinghouse arose in 1713. Mather thought it was too close to his church and withdrew his original promise of support (AB 359). No doubt the younger members of both congregations felt that the old man had lived up to the fear he had expressed in January 1708/9 when he said, "If I dye quickly some few will Lament my death. Whereas if I live awhile longer, age will make me useless" (353). Mather ends his discussion of the meeting house debate by saying testily, "I am perswaded that a blasting from God will be upon them first or last" (359), and he obviously itched to deliver the heavenly chastisement himself.

In April 1714 Mather records the death of his wife, praising her devotion and ability in managing their affairs, and marveling that "[s]he has sayd to many, that She thought I was the best Husband, and the best man in the whole world" (AB 359). Maria Cotton Mather had lived and died in proper Puritan anonymity, and despite the unspoken complaint that in taking Mather's wife first, God had been less than merciful to His faithful servant, her husband left a heart-felt eulogy for their descendants.

At the end of the "Autobiography," Mather admitted defeat in his struggle to influence God's decision regarding a return to England. When he was 76 years old, "the ministers of this province met in Boston by their delegates, and unanimously desired that I would undertake a voyage for England, with an Address from them to the King, praying his Royall favor to these Churches" (AB 359-60). In spite of his age, he was willing to go if his church consented, but "when it was proposed to them, every one of the church lifted up his hand against it" (AB 360). Sadly, he decides that God means him to die in New England. "My Times are in Gods hands; and it is good for me to be where he would have me be" (360), he writes at the end of the "Autobiography," but the words carry more of a sound of resignation than of submission.

Throughout his long life, Increase Mather helped to move New England along its evolutionary path from theocracy to secular state even as he tried to maintain the ways of the past, never recognizing how he himself was changing. In the "Autobiography," he meant to show his descendants how, in "wayting and praying for an earthquake" (AB 320), he had relied on divine providence and so had lived up to the myth of the Founders. Instead, he revealed how he had moved forward from that myth and, in reconstruing divine authority in more personal and political terms, perhaps did more to move New England toward modern ideology than any other figure of his time.

WORKS CITED

"Arguments against relinquishing the Charter." Hutchinson Papers. Collections of the Massachusetts Historical Society. 3rd ser. I: 74-81.

Bercovitch, Sacvan. "New England's Errand Reappraised.J" *New Directions in American Intellectual History.* Ed. John Higham & Paul K. Conkin. Baltimore: Johns Hopkins UP, 1979. 85-104.

Hall, Michael G. *The Last American Puritan: The Life of Increase Mather, 1639-1723.* Middletown: Wesleyan UP, 1988.

Mather, Cotton. "Parentator." *Two Mather Biographies.* Ed. William J. Scheick. Bethlehem: Lehigh UP, 1989.

Mather, Increase. "Autobiography of Increase Mather." Ed. Michael G. Hall. *Proceedings of the American Antiquarian Society,* 71, Part 2, (1961): 271-360.

_____. "Brief Account Concerning Several of the Agents of New England (1691)." *Andros Tracts.* Vol. 3. Boston: Prince Soc., 1869. 272-98. 3 vols.

_____. "Day of Trouble is Near." *Increase Mather: Jeremiads.* Library of American Puritan Writngs, The Seventeenth Century 20. Ser. Ed. Sacvan Bercovitch. New York: AMS Press, 1985. 1-31.

_____. "Life and Death of That Reverend Man of God Mr. Richard Mather." *Two Mather Biographies.* Ed. William J. Scheick. Bethlehem: Lehigh UP, 1989.

_____. "Synod's Work." Williston Walker, *Creeds and Platforms of Congregationalism.* 1893. New York: Pilgrim, 1991. 423-439.

Middlekauff, Robert. *The Mathers: Three Generations of Puritan Intellectuals, 1596-1728.* New York: Oxford UP, 1971.

92

Miller Perry. *Errand into the Wilderness.* Cambridge: Belknap Press of Harvard
UP, 1964.

Murdock, Kenneth B. *Increase Mather: The Foremost American Puritan.*
Cambridge: Harvard UP, 1926.

Shea, Daniel B., Jr. *Spiritual Autobiography in Early America.* Princeton:
Princeton UP, 1988.

Spengemann, William C. & L.R. Lundquist. "Autobiography and the American
Myth." *American Quarterly* 17 (1965)" 501-19.

Stout, Harry S. *New England Soul: Preaching and Religious Culture in Colonial
New England.* New York: Oxford UP, 1986.

White, Eugene E. "Puritan Preaching and the Authority of God." *Preaching in
American History.* Ed. Dewitte Holland. Nashville: Abdingdon, 1969.
36-73.

Intertexuality and Feminist Intervention

in *New Portuguese Letters*

Manuela Mourão

Old Dominion University

Written in 1971 by three women who decided to work together in an effort to denounce the patriarchal structure of Portuguese society and its fascist regime, *New Portuguese Letters* was promptly censored and removed from circulation. The practice of censorship was common in fascist Portugal. The regime's policy of controlling "public morals" was certainly reflected in what books were allowed to be published, what plays could be produced, and what movies could be exhibited. However, the political content of these materials was even more tightly controlled. When the three women, Maria Isabel Barreno, Maria Velho da Costa, and Maria Teresa Horta, were accused of "abuse of the freedom of the press" and "outrage to public decency" (Lane 7) the public was quite aware that the reason behind the government's decision to ban the book and have the writers arrested was political: the work openly attacked the fascist regime and the social inequality it fostered. Moreover, it addressed two of the touchiest issues in the Portuguese society of the seventies--the colonial wars that the country had been waging for nearly fifty years in Angola, Moçambique and Guiné, in an attempt to prevent their independence, and women's rebellion against the constraints imposed upon them by a fierce patriarchal, Catholic society which assigned them the roles of passive and devoted wives and mothers.

When the women were arrested, several international feminist demonstrations protested their detention and brought wide attention to the book. The international scope of the protests was a huge embarrassment for the Portuguese government; still, the trial was prolonged for two years, until a week before the Portuguese Revolution took place.[1] By the time the authors were acquitted and freed, the book had achieved enormous political importance for feminists around the world, as a symbol of sisterhood and resistance. In fact, the first Portuguese feminist organization, known as the **Movement for the Liberation of Woman (Movimento de Libertação da Mulher)**, was formed right after their acquittal, and with their participation.[2] As I will be arguing later, their book was instrumental in contributing to the revolutionary process then taking place in the country.

After renewed critical attention in the 1980's, namely by Linda Kauffman in her book *Discourses of Desire, New Portuguese Letters* became a well-established feminist text; its relevance as a theoretical statement about writing as intervention is, however, far from having been exhausted.[3] Further explored, in light of current feminist preoccupations with postmodernism, this theoretical statement can help us argue for an alliance between the two discourses: as a

---

[1]Linda Kauffman writes that on April 18, 1974, the day before the three writers expected to be sentenced, "the court inexplicably adjourned" (281). The explanation may well be that the first stirrings of the military coup, which a week later on April 25 was to overthrow the fascist regime, were already being felt. The writers still had to stand trial, but they were acquitted.

[2]For the role of the three authors in organizing women, see Kauffman, Wittig and Le Garrec, and Morgan.

[3]In her book, Kauffman has called attention to some of the feminist strategies of *New Portuguese Letters* and has noted how they made the book seem ahead of its time: "What the responses to the *New Portuguese Letters* demonstrated," she states, "was the lack in 1971 of a vocabulary that could encompass the anti-canonical, theoretical, and transgressive strategies of this particular text" (307).

postmodern, feminist text which was conceived in response to a political situation and which incited and inspired political action, *New Portuguese Letters* opens up the possibility to explore how the postmodern can be political and how feminism can benefit from some postmodern tenets.

The book is not easily classifiable in generic terms: it is a collection of narrative texts, poems, and letters, which encompasses but transcends elements of the novel, the feminists tract, the collection of poems, and the scholarly essay. It was conceived as a response to the famous seventeenth-century work of epistolary fiction, *Letters of a Portuguese Nun.*[4] As Kauffman has written, it is "a theoretical text whose very fragmentation is a political posture. . .combin[ing] poetics and politics" (308), where the authors "explore the relations between writing and revolution, between their feminist poetics and global politics" (310). In what is perhaps one of the strongest and most uncompromising explorations of feminist writing as political intervention, *New Portuguese Letters* subverts several traditional literary elements and sheds light on its multiple possibilities for feminine resistance. The authors shape their political project as a "letter" to the nun, but since the book actually resists generic classification because it is constituted by so many different kinds of texts, this can be perceived as a crucial political statement: it implies that systematic feminist scrutiny of patriarchal literary tradition can, in itself, be politically relevant. As it questions patriarchal "certainties," such a scrutiny invites one to contemplate uncertainty and indeterminacy as a process which can lead to the search for an ethics of practice.

---

[4]The *Letters of a Portuguese Nun* appeared anonymously in France during the seventeenth century. Up until recently it had been assumed that this set of five letters had been written by Mariana Alcoforado, a nun in a convent in Beja, the capital of the Portuguese province of Alentejo. The letters were addressed to an officer of the French army stationed in Portugal at the time. It has been established that the letters are a work of fiction written by Guilleragues, a male French author, though possibly based on a real correspondence. The three Marias, however, address the text without mentioning its author, as if to suggest the irrelevance of determining whether the correspondence, the nun, and her lover are "real."

Plurality and indeterminacy, it suggests, may be the only way to ensure that political efforts to effect change do not become fascist in their turn. *New Portuguese Letters* is thus a powerful illustration of the potential for success of a politics of the uncertain.[5] As the writers initially confront their desire for unity and finally accept the need for difference, the book urges us to be cautious and reflexive, to resist the drive to erase tensions and ambivalences, and opens up the space for many voices to be heard. Indeed, in its awareness of the need to acknowledge difference and confront tensions, this long "letter" not only transcends literary genres, but also cuts across culture, gender, and social class. The characters of the different narratives, the speakers of the various poems and letters, and the three implied authors ensure a non-essentialist perspective that actually increases the work's effectiveness as political intervention.

The complexity of the work's transtextuality, which Gérard Genette has defined as "everything that puts the text in an obvious or secret relation with other texts" (119)[6], adds to its already considerable representation of diversity" to all the different voices in this work are added other voices form other works making us aware of the historical continuum of oppression and resistance.[7]

---

[5]In her essay "The Pirate's Fiancée: Feminist Philosophers, or maybe tonight it will happen," Meaghan Morris talks about "a politics of the provisional and the definitely uncertain" (21), an expression which I think perfectly expresses the project of this work.

[6]My translation.

[7]The Portuguese nun, though the main voice invoked here, is by no means the only important symbol of female oppression. Among others, the lives of Ophelia, Jeanne d'Arc, and Dona Inês de Castro are celebrated, and their deaths lamented in three poems (184-6). Elizabeth Barrett Browning's voice is also evoked in two poems from her *Sonnets from the Portuguese* (299-300). And in a long section of the book a host of women, real and fictional characters, cited in Collin de Plancy's *Dictionnaire de Sorcellerie,* are remembered for the persecutions they suffered: the Bloodstained Nun, who killed her lover; Maria de la Ralde, who was accused of sorcery; Louise Maillat, who was exorcised; Gabrielle d'Estrées, mistress of Henry IV; Cecilia, a sixteenth-century Portuguese ventriloquist accused of sorcery and banished from the country; and Marie de Marguerite de

Besides considering social and cultural diversity and gender difference, the feminist political project advanced by this work attempts to identify all the levels of oppression that permeate each of these structures. By depicting how in different political struggles of class and gender the strategies of patriarchal and Fascist domination are utilized, the authors offer a powerful critique of how the oppressed may oppress in turn, and help perpetuate oppression and exploitation. One text in particular dramatizes this: "Duties," a writing exercise by a primary school girl. The little girl focuses on "two main kinds of duties: men's duties, and women's duties (301). As she addresses the situation of her own family--her father's duty is to exercise authority and her mother's is to obey him--Adelia demonstrates how the instruments of oppression are not only the patriarchal institutions and the fascist regime which endorses them as means of oppression, but also those who unconsciously use them, conform to them, and are victimized by them: her father is oppressed and exploited at the factory, but he oppresses and exploits her mother, who in turn oppresses Adelia. What she has learned form this is that she needs to marry a rich man who can provide her with "nice dresses, a car, and two maids" (302).

The attention to the intersection of all these elements notwithstanding, the authors admit that this project can be potentially oppressive. Despite the fact that they explicitly decenter the text and take a nonhierarchical stance to political intervention, they are aware of, and often alert the reader to, the complexity of representing the various "others" in an ideal, nonhierarchical manner. This self-consciousness about their potential role as leaders, or as it were, dictators of the rules for "liberation," is one of the most striking elements of the work. As we will see, however, their caution, rather than producing paralysis, actually transforms the work into a valuable study of how "to multiply, rather than restrict, the points from which women's struggle can develop" (Morris 39).

Branvilliers, who was burned at the stake after having been accused of poisoning, symbolize patriarchal fear and containment of women throughout history.

New Portuguese Letters is, therefore, the kind of text that begs to be included in a discussion of the possibility of an alliance between postmodernism and feminism: it can help us explore whether "postmodernism, because it rejects absolute values, cannot provide a viable political program" (Hekman 6), or whether "a political of the provisional and the definitely uncertain" (Morris 21) can lead to "resistance to whatever form totalitarian power might take" (Diamond xiii). Since, in matters of theory, a discussion of specific works often proves more revealing than one confined to abstract theoretical terms, this paper means to contribute to the feminism/postmodernism debate by analyzing how the project of *New Portuguese Letters* actually illustrates the potential for an alliance of the two discourses. As I will argue, *New Portuguese Letters* shows that not only is political intervention consistent with a postmodern feminism, but--as Hekman and others have insisted--a postmodern stance can actually solve some of the political problems of contemporary feminism: by challenging dichotomies, by rejecting essentialism, and by striving toward a nonhierarchical representation of diversity, *New Portuguese Letters* combines feminist political intervention and a philosophical preoccupation with rejecting absolute values that is clearly postmodern. Politically radical, this work suggests the possibility of a postmodern feminism which need not lose its primary vocation of political intervention. Since the most common feminist objections to postmodern philosophy are its alleged prevention of political commitment and its rejection of "truth," it is important to demonstrate how, in *New Portuguese Letters*, the systematic denunciation of the "truths" that are authorized and fostered by patriarchal ideology actually constitutes political intervention and highlights the common ground between feminist and postmodern critiques.[8]

---

[8]Since the end of the 1980's, there has been a consistent preoccupation, on the part of several feminist theorists, to argue for an alliance between feminism and postmodernism. See, for example, Diamond and Quinby, Hekman, and Nicholson. Barbara Creed has also stressed the common ground shared by feminism and postmodernism.

* * *

We will start by analyzing how the intertextual relations make the text resist being classified in terms of genre, and how that resistance is problematized.[9] As the preface of the translator points out, the authors maintained that '*What* is in the book cannot be dissociated from *how* it evolved' (8). It started as a series of poems, narrative texts, and essays about the condition of women that the three authors composed to discuss at regular meetings. When the idea of turning these pieces into a book emerged, the women chose to organize them as a response to the seventeenth-century nun. Thus, the book started to take shape as a collection of pieces written weekly, dated but unsigned, and of letters that each author decided to write to the other two, either commenting on the project--and here, again, we have an element of postmodern self-reflexivity--or discussing personal issues. Gradually, the scope of the material widened and the authors experimented with the epistolary form, creating "fictitious seventeenth-century letters developing the Mariana Alcoforado theme" (401); letters "to and from a long line of Mariana's female descendants and their lovers, spanning a period of three centuries;" letters "written by a host of fictitious Marias and Marianas and Maria Anas of today" (11); and "fictitious letters on such contemporary national themes as emigration, repression, war overseas, [as well as] feminine and masculine roles" (401).[10]

---

[9]That a text which consistently breaks established notions of genre may constitute in itself another genre is, of course, a notion that immediately arises. The authors themselves address this paradox: they know they are doing something new, and yet are also conscious that there is nothing new in trying to do something new. The paradoxical element, which arises from the text's problematization of its own oppositional stance, and which I identify as a postmodern characteristic, also manifests itself, for example, in how the text is at once self-reflexive and intertextual, and in how it is both a collection of letters between different characters and a letter to the seventeenth-century nun.

[10]Even though the letters span a period of three centuries, the issues they address are, again and again, the oppression and discrimination that women have suffered throughout history. The names, all variants of the name Mariana, are

Their choice of title allowed them to appropriate the epistolary genre, traditionally the one literary venue open to women,[11] and to stress the degree to which the work functions intertextually. Their choice to add poetry, fiction, and essays suggests both a desire to transgress the very notion of letter writing as women's only appropriate sphere in literature, and to transgress the traditional boundaries between genres in order to create a text which, in its plurality, would accommodate the representation of female experience and multiply the possibilities for female resistance.

A result of this subversive impulse, the work's collage-like quality is instrumental in creating the text's many voices and in ensuring that issues of gender, class, and cultural difference are raised from several different perspectives and remain in tension, rather than being resolved.[12] The authors consistently problematize closure and question the desirability of a unified theory of resistance, intervention, or political change. These provisional and tentative qualities in the text, which mark it as postmodern, resist a literary tradition that privileges closure; thus, they illustrate how, to an extent, the literary can consciously make a transition to the political, and that the postmodern qualities of the text do not prevent it.

In the "Afterword" the authors discuss how their resistance took shape:

---

a way to stress this repetition as well as the fact that in three centuries what is at the core of women's oppression has not changed. The different historic contexts and social classes in which the lives of these women unfold are considered but are represented as ultimately less relevant than their condition as women: dissatisfaction, rebellion, madness, or suicide is the lot of most of them.

[11]For studies of epistolarity and women writers see Robert Adams Day, François Jost, Dale Spender, and perhaps the most interesting in this context, Elizabeth J. MacArthur.

[12]Fredric Jameson, in his essay "Postmodernism, Or, The Cultural Logic of Late Capitalism," identifies pastiche and schizophrenia as crucial traits of postmodernism. This text, with its collage=like quality and its multiple voices, exhibits both elements, since it suggests a decentered subject.

> We set ourselves no rules as to style, literary genres, quantity
> . . . . Things in it presented as they came. . .the THING pulsing
> with a life of its own, from beginning to end, since otherwise we
> could and would be engulfed by it, possessed by it, and in the end
> perhaps too tired, too frightened to carry it further. (401)

A work which attempts to resist patriarchy must, above all, break its rules: their principles of literary production defy traditional ones and successfully transgress patriarchal norms of literary craft. As *New Portuguese Letters* becomes a practice, (rather than a theory) of resistance, it suggests that the text can be constituted as the site of that resistance.[13] Indeed, the writers' refusal to conform to the norms and limitations traditionally implicit in any genre suggests, as Irigaray has theorized, that they are constituting their writing as "a [specific] site of resistance and liberation in [a] phallocentric universe" (Jones 85). As she maintains, writing can be instrumental in women's attempt to escape the phallocentric universe: "If women have been entrapped in the symbolic order," she writes, "they will make their escape from it by producing texts that challenge and move beyond the Law-of-the-Father" (Jones 85).[14] *New Portuguese Letters* attempts to do just that; however, it is important to stress that it is not simply by virtue of equating experimental writing with an essentially feminine and/or feminist impulse that this is attempted. *New Portuguese Letters* is a work where

---

[13]If this is a notion that most feminists today accept as a given, we should remember that *New Portuguese Letters* was being written about the same time that Cixous and Irigaray started to explore language's potential for challenging patriarchy and to theorize the notion of *écriture feminine*. This is a case of "practice and its demands precede[ing] theory," which as Nancy K. Miller rightly stresses in *Subject to Change* "historically has been the case with feminism (68).

[14]According to French theories of the feminine, women are absent as subjects from phallocentric discourses such as philosophy and psychoanalysis. "Woman must put herself into the text," writes Cixous in "The Laugh of the Medusa" (cited in Jones 85). Through "feminine writing" women can constitute themselves as subjects and resist phallocentrism. In *New Portuguese Letters* we witness a version of that process taking place as the three women writers challenge the rules of patriarchal literary tradition.

politics encompasses but is not limited to a textual practice; rather, it specifically and systematically connects the transgressive nature of its formal features to its thematic concern with the political goals of feminism.[15] Since these formal features openly resist taxonomy, they also challenge ordinary reading practices: the writer's conscious act of transgressing classical genre theory forces the readers to question traditional (patriarchal) laws of genre, and to consider the implications of that transgression as a political statement.

Because the feminist political project of *New Portuguese Letters* relies, in part, on the authors' refusal to accommodate feminist theory and feminine experience to traditional critical models, the very rich and complex relationships between this work and other tests are the very core of the critique. By exploring intertextual, metatextual, paratextual, and architextual[16] relationships with the seventeenth-century text, the authors make their work a citation of, a critical comment on, and an imitation and transformation of *Letters of a Portuguese Nun*. Most notably, they consistently expand its architextuality, that is, "its relation to the different types of discourse form which it springs--the different genres and

---

[15]Rita Felski, in *Beyond Feminist Aesthetics,* argues that "[I]t is impossible to make a convincing case for the claim that there is anything inherently feminine or feminist in experimental writing as such" (5). Therefore, she finds French feminist theories limited in their identification "of the (usually experimental) text as a privileged site of resistance to patriarchal ideology by virtue of its subversion of the representation and instrumental function of symbolic discourse" (4). *New Portuguese Letters*, however, is a text about which this claim is justified, not only because of the obvious political motivation of such a textual practice, but also because of the very practical political results it had. In pre-revolutionary Portugal of the early 1970's, where organized resistance to fascism existed only underground, this text contributed to bring to open forum urgent political issues. Once the revolution took place, *New Portuguese Letters* became the catalyst for organized feminist action--for, it must be stressed, the military officers that led the *coup* did nothing to make women's issues a priority in their political programs. That women seized the moment and organized is definitely due, in part, to the three authors and their book.

[16]For these terms see Genette.

their determined characteristics, formal, thematic, and others" (Genette 119). Their feminist critique is thus equated with an exploration of textual relations which is far form remaining on a purely theoretical or abstract level. By engaging with literary tradition at both the formal and the thematic levels, and by engaging with a specific text whose reception has been historically relevant to an understanding of the representation of female passion and female submission,[17] the authors define the act of writing as intervention at a very specific level.

Even though they repeatedly posit writing as revision as one of the main possibilities for feminist intervention--as is clear form the number of letters they include "by" and "to" Mariana Alcoforado--they do not see this as unproblematic. Their question, "My sisters:/ But what can literature do? Or rather what can words do?" (266), reflects the problem of a feminist practice rooted int he textual which aims to go beyond the theoretical and the abstract. Since they question their own right to exercise control or authority, they do not wish to solve the problem through didacticism or through transforming their work into a manifesto.

Their determination to ignore the traditional authorial claim--they do not sign any of the parts of the work they are individually responsible for, therefore each individual contribution to the book cannot be attributed to a specific woman--is connected to their understanding of writing as political analysis and political intervention: on the one hand, and in very practical terms, it was safer for them, in the context of fascist Portugal, to remain anonymous; on the other hand, their anonymity helps them refrain from exercising "authority," an issue which they repeatedly problematize. Clearly, then, this surrender of the authorial right to "control" the text, to attempt to establish a meaning, becomes yet another feminist political statement: the individuality of every voice in the text is emphasized while the politics of the relationship between the different social classes or genders is

---

[17]For important feminist readings of *Letters of a Portuguese Nun* which address the issue of female passion and female submission, see Kamuf and Kauffman.

dramatized. An example among many is a letter from a woman named Maria Ana to her husband, an emigrant residing in Canada:

> My beloved and never forgotten António I am taking advantage of our cousin Luisa's visit to me today to send you this letter that she's kindly offered to write for me to you how much I miss hearing from you. Listen António you haven't been back to see us for two years now and this only makes things worse even though youre (sic) very good about sending money--our Jorge cashes your money orders in Aveiro every month and may Our Lord repay you for working so hard and your children and I are very grateful to you. . .The land we already have is more than enough and Ive (sic) bought still more Amelia's husband helps till it when he isn't drunk but the only thing that will grow in it is brambles and briars because the waters of the Caima are filthy and as you saw when you were here it made all the fish die not to mention the beans, so all the money I've spent on land has gone to waste, and the paper factory is still the only place where there's work for anybody who stays around here till he's called up for military service. . . .I'm embroidering things and making the house look nice for your return even though I don't have any idea whether you really will come back. (150-1)[18]

By emphasizing the individuality of these different voices, rather than stressing the narrator's or the implied author's control, the authors become as much part of the drama as their characters. They do comment on the project, raise problems, and suggest strategies, but their voices are not comparable to the voices of traditional reliable narrators; as a result, their power to facilitate the emergence of one particular meaning over another is not noticeably greater than that of any of the characters. Far from offering the illusion of a unified, regulated meaning,

---

[18]The region around Aveiro is still an area from which men are mostly absent and where women raise their children alone. Because work in the fields is not lucrative, due, among other things, to the pollution caused by the paper factory, many men either emigrate to Canada and to the United States, or join the crews of cod fishing ships that stay in the North Atlantic for up to six month at a time. This letter problematizes women's economic dependence on men and their lonely struggle to raise a family fragmented because of economical and military reasons. These questions still reflect the reality of the working classes in Portuguese society.

the three authors ensure that conflict and ambiguity remain. A letter between two friends, one of whom is fighting in the colonies, illustrates this:

> Like I promised I would, I'm sending you a few lines to tell you what to expect if you ever land in these parts, which could be better, I must say, because when we go out on mission we find ourselves slogging through mud up to our balls and it's hard going with our heavy weapons, not to mention the fear of being ambushed. The other day there was a guy who got his nuts shot off. . . .They say you have to accept your lot in life, but I just can't resign myself to the prospect of staying here for so many years. . . .There's no lack of women, but as you know I'm not really the kind to go in for that sort of thing, and besides, I'm scared of catching some disease form them because all of the other guys sleep with them. Some of the chicks are quite good-looking, with nice, firm, bare-naked tits, and sometimes you get so crazy in the head you couldn't care less what they smell like or what color they are. . .we're all the same, I know. . .but it upsets me and I keep thinking about these things after I screwed them. . . .
>
> [Joana] doesn't want us to get married now--'It's better to end the whole thing,' she says in her letters. . . .She's putting on airs now that she's got herself an education and it seems I'm no good for her any more because at one point I said to your mother . . . 'Let her learn dressmaking if she's in such frail health and thinks she's too good to work in the fields the rest of her life. I'm not in favor of her getting an education' (241-2).

As the two examples show, the text literally flaunts plurality as numerous perspectives are dramatized. Being "at odds" is a positive political stance insofar as it is a sign of self-sufficiency and of freedom:

> I tell you, sisters, you with whom I have begun to be so secretly at odds. . . .If a person is not self-sufficient. . .let him or her above all laugh. . .until he or she *is* self-sufficient. . . .Nor is there another formula for liberation from anything (358).

This writer confesses her disagreement with the other two. If, initially, she kept her disagreement secret, she soon came to regard it as a sign of freedom. The ambivalence towards difference remains until the end of the book, but dissent is represented as an act both of transgression and freedom, and unequivocally indicates that the writers advocate plurality:

> the terrible difference between us at first. . . .A difference that

> was not healed, though our exercise was a sort of soothing balm
> that alleviated it somewhat. . . .Look at the difference now, after
> working so hard for a unity we never quite succeeded in achieving.
> Look at how in these final pages we are again donning our masks--
> the masks that once upon a time fitted so well (384).

As these word show, *New Portuguese Letters* is far from offering a single, fixed

analysis of female nature or feminist resistance. At one point the writers had

yearned for unity and strived for consensus, but eventually they realized that this

entailed "donning . . . masks" for the sake of sisterhood.

Related to this struggle against the impulse to smooth away difference is

the struggle against the impulse to assume a privileged position. They know that

despite their act of denunciation, their voices, like all other voices in the book,

are in danger of remaining entrapped in patriarchal discourse. The question as

it is formulated by the three writers is, then, how to attain change. Repeatedly,

the authors question the effectiveness of their writing: "(I understand, you

understand, he understands, we all understand the situation, in the beginning was

the Word, and there we remained waiting for the creative power of words, their

power to change things, to come our way)" (372). And later on:

> I've grown tired of words now that you insist on using them as
> substitutes for actions. . . .For you it is not simply a question of
> putting words together, I know. . .[but] we have filled reams of
> paper over the months, and what can we do, what are we doing?
> . . . you fail to show the difference between the prose you sweat
> over and that delicate, sophisticated, highly stylized lacework of
> words that betrays how distant the Other is from you despite your
> genuine concern. . . .[T]o you, protest becomes bullshit that sells
> posters. So you make games and rocking horses out of words. . .
> haven't you made sheer garbage out of words (377)?

By bringing into question the political validity of their writing, they stress their

understanding of the gap between each one of us. Moreover, they hint at how

close one can always be to mistaking writing as aesthetic pleasure for writing as

genuine intervention.

A consistent search for how writing can become intervention is, they

suggest, part of the process. The opening lines of the book equate writing with passion, offering an insight into what they search for:

> . . .Granted, then, that all of literature is a long letter to an
> invisible other, a present, a possible, or a future passion that we
> rid ourselves of, feed, or seek. We have also agreed that what is
> of interest is not so much the object of our passion, which is a
> mere pretext, but passion itself; to which I add that what is of
> interest is not so much passion itself, which is a mere pretext, but
> its exercise. (15).

Writing is the exerciser of passion. And their engagement with a feminine literary tradition links the act of writing as personal with the act of writing as a meaningful political, feminist intervention. This is clear in "Third Letter I":

> Ponder the fact, my sisters. . .that this literary novelty of ours is
> going to sell well. . . . Think about what I told you--it's like the
> sun: it's for us and for others. Think about the contract proposed,
> the shattered cloister walls we would disclose. . .there is always
> a cloister awaiting whoever proudly defies custom and tradition:
> a nun does not copulate
> a woman who has borne children and earned a diploma
> writes but does not overcome obstacles
> (and certainly not in a sisterhood of three)
> through Literature. . .
> how many problems I foresee, sister: the three of us will be
> considered a single case, though we have no way of knowing if it
> will become a cause, and for that very reason we give each other
> our hands, and hold them onto others. (20-1)

Their writing is intervention insofar as it "shatters cloister walls" and insofar as they "hold [their hands] onto (sic) others." It becomes part of a feminine/feminist writing tradition, because it resuscitates all the feminine voices that have historically been suppressed and incorporates them into their political project. As such, their writing acquires the political meaning they hoped for:

> (I ask:
> Sisters, how many Anas or Marianas must still be brought back to
> life, or how many of them are still living who are being put to the
> test, having their minds dulled, made weak and fragile through the
> working of the law, the social proprieties, accepted beliefs, and
> religion?) (328)

As this excerpt stresses, the fight against oppression is tied to the bringing back to life, through literature, of the voices of women who have denounced that oppression or been its victims. The political relevance of the writers' determination to ignore the tradition authorial claim is again apparent: their work is part of a continuum of female writing and one among the many voices which the text's intertextuality allows them to evoke.

* * *

As we have seen, *New Portuguese Letters'* challenge of genre and authorial control is an essential strategy in constituting writing as intervention. This challenge is further more coupled with a thematic treatment that emphasizes the spirit of feminist intervention of the work and reaffirms the possibility of a transition form the literary to the political: the book explicitly addresses women's oppression. Its feminist political project becomes, at the semantic level, ostensibly connected with subversion: by appropriating and subverting patriarchal representations of women, *New Portuguese Letters* puts to use the political potential of the instability of meaning.

The nun is the central metaphor. Through her different representations, the subversive potential of this instability will be played out. Specifically, in answering the seventeenth-century nun, the authors rewrite her story; they challenge the traditional interpretation of the nun as a heart-broken lover who had been abandoned and offer several other alternatives for reading her letters to the chevalier. Derrida's concept of *différance* is crucial for this reading of *New Portuguese Letters*: rather that substituting one reading for another, the authors ensure that the concept of the "nun" and the "reality " of Mariana remain unstable and, thus, open. The potential for additional meaning that can be used for political purposes, even if transitory, is maintained.

Kauffman suggests as much when she stresses that the "intertextual dynamics between this text and the *Letters of a Portuguese Nun* depends on a logic of relations and analogy" that leads to "open-ended discoveries" (298); the authors consistently resist closure. This strategy, I would argue, creates the instability of meaning essential for a political intervention that rejects essentialism. By challenging accepted meanings of the seventeenth-century text which define the nun as a faithful lover, pleading with a man who has deserted her, the authors delineate a feminist political project that creates spaces within which the reinterpretation of the traditional fictional representation of nuns and women can be situated.[19] Their re-reading process reframes and recenters the text and ultimate reaffirms the empowerment of the act of appropriating and subverting patriarchal representations of women. Such a process illustrates what a postmodern feminist critical practice could be: one that can resist many political agendas by virtue of its intertextuality and its resistance to closure: in their reading of *Letters of a Portuguese Nun* we can see Mariana resisting the patriarchal laws that make a nun of every woman, as well as the specific fascist regime in Portugal in 1971.

For a clear display of the process of subversion at the semantic level in *New Portuguese Letters* we will concentrate on letters between Mariana and her lover, the chevalier de Chamilly, and on a few poems and sketches that specifically concern her. It is through these that the three writers re-invent the nun. As has been noted, in the traditional readings of the seventeenth-century text Mariana is seen exclusively as a lovelorn woman. Readers were much taken by her seemingly prodigious capacity for love and suffering. The letters excited general attention because they were believed to be authentic and to represent a woman's excess of love overcoming her pride and her dignity: "From the first moment I saw you my life was yours, and somehow I take pleasure in sacrificing it to you" (|Guilleragues 403), the first letter reads. Her passion was a spectacle and she was lamented and admired in her constancy to an unfaithful lover.[20]

---

[19]See my "Nun's Stories, Nuns' Voices: Resistance at the Margins of Patriarchal Ideology," for a sustained analysis of traditional fictional representations of nuns.

[20]For a recent study of the reception of the seventeenth-century text, see Isabelle Landy-Houillon.

The texts we will analyze displace this representation. They do not offer a unified representation of the nun which either endorses or contradicts the traditional image of Mariana; rather, they offer several possible versions of Mariana, each one as probable as the other. These different versions allow us to explore the political relevance, for feminism, of displacing traditional meanings of woman. Since the various representations of Mariana are constructed through the writings of the different correspondents, the extent to which each "version" of the nun is constituted by, and thus dependent on, the different subjectivities of each of the writers of the letters and poems is stressed. This, in turn, allows the authors to uncover the ideological nature of representation, thus stressing the role of (their) writing as intervention.

The poem entitled "Song of Mariana Alcoforado to Her Mother" is the first text in the book to engage in a specific attempt to represent the nun. The "version" of Mariana it starts to construct is that of an unhappy woman who desperately resents being in the convent. The speaker of the poem is Mariana herself. Addressing her mother, the nun makes clear that she knows she was not a wanted child. The relationship between mother and daughter is represented as increasingly painful: as the poem progresses, pain gives way to remoteness and the mother/child bond ceases to exist. Conception is described through an image of the child as a kind of parasite, or a disease: "I gnawed at your vitals/tricked into entering them" (72). Birth is raw pain, unmediated by any feeling of joy:

O immensely painful fate
O my remembered labor
O its intense agony
O your delivery long past term
fear sadness and support
your shoulder of my earliest days. (72)

The increasing distance between mother and daughter leaves painful traces:

Absence become as bruising
as a stone set in a ring
squeezing a finger. (72)

And her forced entry into the convent is seen as proof of her mother's indifference:

> For daughter put in a convent
> is not loved in her house. (72)

The poem ends with the equation of this childbearing experience to emptiness:

> Madam my mother, you who found yourself
> with child
> without knowing it
> seeing your belly swell
>
> without feeling yourself
> inhabited. (73)

Another poem, "Ballad by Mariana Alcoforado in the Manner of a Lament," complicates this image of Mariana. She is still represented as unhappy and the convent is still seen as a prison, but several images of emptiness and alienation suggest that she has not resigned herself:

> They looked upon me as a nun
> resigned to
> the habit that cloak myself in
> or once inhabited
> . . . .They consider me a prisoner by law
> offered in sacrifice
> yet I freed myself. (85)

Even though Mariana sees the future as lost ("The lost days I have yet to live/crowd in upon me/ and cloister walls I never broke"), the refrain, repeated five times, suggests a certain defiance:

> how distant I was
> so distant from myself (86).

In "Lament of Mariana Alcoforado for Dona Brites," Mariana bares her soul to her friend Dona Brites, another nun. The lament adds to the ambiguity of Mariana by addressing the very issue of her representation: "Everyone has always had such a biased or distorted view of my entire life," she says, "[b]ut never have I felt as lost, as trapped by others, as eager to deceive everyone in every way within my power" (104). The passage suggests that Mariana's "reality," fixed by its seventeenth-century literary representations, is to be questioned as the nun repeatedly invents herself. Readers are prevented form indulging in certainty: they must confront a set of possible "realities" spun by the different representations of herself that Mariana purposefully leaves ambiguous. Thus the laments that follow, as well as the images of despair and near madness, have already been brought into question. As they unfold, it is not possible to determine for sure who Mariana is. First, we are confronted with Mariana self-alienated:

> I have been distracted and distant from myself for years now. But how can one bear to grow old if there is nothing left to cling to . . . .I have turned into stone to engender stone, and when I run my fingers, my tongue, over these walls, what I taste and feel is roughness, a cold emptiness. . . .I would be so happy to die that I doubt that death can overtake me soon enough. (104)

Second, we see Mariana nearly mad with despair:

> I stretch my bare arms outside my cell: how cold the bars are, and how high the window is. . . .How may times have you wrenched me away: stiff, rigid, naked, my arms uplifted, stretched outside the window, and my face raw form rubbing it, in tears, against the rough wall. . . .I cry out in pain, tearing the pillowcase and biting it, as I bite my arms. (105-7)

Third, we become aware of her passionate hatred:

> Only my burning passion raises my spirits, and my sudden accesses of hatred under cover of night. . .even the garments I wear have been forced upon me. . .How may times have you yourself very nearly forced me bodily into donning them yet another day? (106)

Finally, we are confronted with her intense yearning for life and for the world:

> [T]his convent need have no fear of my excesses, it is only I who suffer from them, I gather them up within myself and they come forth from me though every part of my body, every one of my deserted places. Of what interest to her is this yearning of mine for the world, this dizzying pull of the earth, this will of mine to drink the sea (to drain it Reverend Mother, to the very last drop), this mad forgotten craving to touch all things that wander in order to grasp them firmly in my hand. My life will ebb away little by little, Reverend Mother, if I do not express my longings, if I neither fulfill them nor take my vengeance for them. (106-7)

All of these representations are equally strong: the three authors develop their character through fictions of herself created by herself, and no one fiction is more valid than another. Thus, skillfully, Mariana's identity is maintained elusive, indeterminable, or at least unfixable.

This play of meaning is intensified by the correspondence between the nun and the chevalier. The first letter she writes to him, in which she hints at the possibility of being pregnant, suggests that she is not aware of having been abandoned. She feels that the chevalier's ardor has diminished and somewhat resentfully, somewhat apologetically, somewhat hopefully, she uses all she can to make him come to her:

> Forgive me for writing you even though I know--my reason and my heart tell me so--how relieved you feel each time you leave my side . . . . Why, my love, this silence you swear me to . . . a silence that I anxiously devour? If I do not take my sustenance from you, what fate awaits me?
>
> Forgive these frantic ravings; forgive my anxiety. . . .I am prey to worse and worse fears with each passing day, not knowing how to resolve a situation that I should not rightfully be obliged to solve by myself.
>
> I shall therefore expect you tonight. You may rest assured that I shall not vex you with wearisome floods of tears or warm embraces. I shall avoid, my love, I swear to you, supplications, irony, fond reminiscences. (76-7)

In this letter to her lover, Mariana's voice is that of a passionate and wronged lover. This conforms to the traditional understanding of her character as that of a woman who deserves pity for having been abandoned and admiration for remaining constant in her love for an unworthy man. Indeed, in this passage the three authors are drawing on the history of the reception of the seventeenth-century *Letters*, but only to question its validity since the chevalier's response to Mariana's pleas will problematize the woman constructed by the earlier representation:[21]

---

[21]The absolute furor around the letters was mostly due to the intensity of feeling they exhibited. The spectacle of the woman's passion was so compelling

> Keep the respect that you owe yourself.
> Love is better served by dignity than by complaints and lies. Remember that I am too well acquainted, out of experience, with your excesses, your sudden fits of rage, and your caprices. It will be best for both of us if I depart, turning a deaf ear to your tricks and stratagems and refusing to believe you capable of them, for they ill become you. (82)

The chevalier's words add to the play of ambiguity which Mariana's self-representation has been maintaining. His reading of her adds another layer of possible meaning to her elusive identity: in sharp contrast to the picture of the bereaved, lovelorn woman constructed by the poems and by her first letter, Mariana is here represented as a capricious deceiver. At this point, the text is clearly underscoring the degree to which Mariana's "reality" is interpreted differently depending on the subjectivities of those reading her. That this is the reading prompted by the subjectivity of the man who has abandoned her suggests, furthermore, that Mariana's refusal to conform to the chevalier's expectations makes her "unreadable" to him. The text constructs Mariana's resistance to patriarchal pressure--as a woman, a nun, and a lover--as too complex for the chevalier to understand. His response is to reduce her to an unspeakably false and dangerous character, constructing himself as a victim of her wiles.

The letter further exhibits his intense fear of her sexuality. Indeed, it is Mariana's "excessive" passion that is at the root of the chevalier's vehement indictment:

> And if you invoke love and passion, what proofs of passion did you ever give me, save that for yourself, fanning its devouring flames to serve your own aims and purposes?
> Senhora, be on your guard against yourself, for everything about you is poison; protect yourself from yourself as I protect myself for you and ride away, overcome with astonishment at encountering so much malice and hatred and selfishness in a single woman. (82)

---

that responses and imitation proliferated. See Jost and Landy-Houillon, already cited.

Because the object of Mariana's passion is passion itself, rather than the lover, he perceives her as dangerous. The degree to which he fears her sexuality is even more obvious in the following passage:

> You were a virgin when I first took you, yet I had never known a woman who had reached such depraved heights of sensuality, mad ecstasy, frenetic desire. You had me in your power, as you knew full well--suffering from your fever, which set my body on fire. . . .

> Do not trouble yourself further: you will never see me again. I am fleeing you and willingly confess that I am doing so without the least remorse, since I am well aware of how you used me for your own ends without ever wholly surrendering yourself to me. (83)

Because Mariana indulged in passion for passion's sake, because she held the satisfaction of her desire dearer than the chevalier's and used him without surrendering herself, he sees her as a monster. His fear is compounded by his awareness of her intelligence, which he deems "vast, and, indeed, excessive in a woman" (84).

The chevalier's representation of Mariana as a woman who is dangerous because she is passionate, intelligent, and insubmissive introduces, then, a new element in a text which already contains plural possibilities. Through her self-representation, Mariana, in all her elusiveness, had remained suggestively the victim. The chevalier's intervention invites the reader to re-evaluate this notion and contemplate another possible reading of the nun; her elusive identity remains unfixable.

The chevalier's only other letter, dated Good Friday of 1671, in which he announces to her that he has had her letters published, also draws on the history of the reception of the seventeenth-century *Letters:* first, it alludes directly to the story of the publication of the seventeenth-century text; then, it alludes to its success. Because of this direct reference, it allows for a considerable degree of intertextual play at the semantic level. Indeed, by having the chevalier refer so directly to the seventeenth-century text, the writers inevitably evoke the meanings of Mariana that traditionally had been attached to it: a jilted woman, European society had pitied her and admired her endless capacity for love. Instability is therefore the more successfully achieved when, by contrast, the chevalier represents Mariana as a calculating, cold woman who used him:

> Her Majesty the Queen is enjoying [your letters] in secret, everyone finds you charming, Marianne, you have attained your goal, you are now bound within the pages of a book that gives promise of being world renowned and been crowned a clever, talented woman, a woman of the world. There is hence no further reason for you to use me as a pretext for your grief-stricken outpourings, to make me the pretended cause of your suffering (121).

Chamilly's impression that he has been used corresponds to an important element in the seventeenth-century text: by the time she writes her last letter, Mariana has discovered that her passion, rather than the loss of the lover, is what is important to her. When, in the previous passage, the chevalier writes that there is no further reason for Mariana to use him as a pretext, we are reminded of the nun's reproaches, in the early text, for his letting her know that he no longer cares. Her fear is that such frankness might contribute to kill her passion--all that matters to her now:

> I discovered that it was not so much you as my own passion to which I was attached. . . . You with your frankness--how I despise it. Have I ever implored you to tell me the truth? Why did you not leave me my illusions? You needed only to stop writing. (Guillerages 423)

Drawing on an interpretation of these lines which valorizes the self-serving side of the nun's excess of emotion, the authors construct yet another possible Mariana: in the rest of his letter, the chevalier offers an image of his lover as frivolous, detached and pleasure seeking. Whatever the intensity of her emotions, the chevalier is not their center:

> this letter will remain among my papers, so that one day. . . it may justify me, not for having abandoned you, for I never left you, Senhora, but for feeling so aggrieved at your aloofness, since I have served as the pretext and the object of writings and feelings that should never have existed. (126-7)

And the letter closes with a suggestion that the nun's writing came to be the source of her emotional fulfillment. Her excess of emotion, the intense grief and the enduring passion, were cultivated as a pretext for writing:

> . . .you have turned your belated tears into an elegantly polished tale of blighted courtly love. . . .I am very much aware, through your letter and your art, that the talent you have given proof of in composing them is the talent that has always been yours alone: that of finding happiness in every possible way of freeing yourself of all constraints. (126-7)

In the "Sixth and Final Letter from Dona Mariana Alcoforado, a Nun in Beja, to the Chevalier de Chamilly, Written on Christmas Day of the Year of Grace 1671," the authors further explore this image of the nun cultivating her emotions, detached form their object, in order to attain personal fulfillment through writing about them. That this is the sixth letter is significant: the Portuguese nun only sent five letters to her French lover, refraining from sending a sixth one because of having realized that he no longer loved her. Yet, she may have written many more, which is precisely what the authors suggest as Mariana starts letter six with the words "It is not my intention to ever send you these lines to read, for their sole purpose is to be committed to paper" (342). Mariana, the letter suggests, is using writing for her own sake for she has discovered that the act of writing to the lover is a more powerful experience than loving him has ever been:

> I wrote you letters full of great love and great torment, Senhor, and after having had no commerce with you for so long, I began to love them and the act of writing about them more than I loved your image or the memory of you. I have penned many more missives than I have cared to send you, for this was a way of taking pleasure in the act of writing. (342)

By developing Mariana's understanding of the role of writing in her construction of herself, the authors offer an image of the nun as a woman who has a considerable amount of power. The degree to which writing allows Mariana to increase control over her personal reality is notable; moreover, it effectively convinces her of the essential inadequacy of patriarchal discourse as the vehicle of her self-representation(s). This empowering realization is stressed in her words to her ex-lover:

> And so it was that by writing and by reading. . .I came to understand, Senhor, that I had composed nothing that had not already been expressed. . . .And it was then that I began to smile at my sorrows, since what was really mine, really genuine about them I had never contrived to set down in words, and it now seems to me that for what is really true there are no words. . . . Hence I am beginning to ask myself whether I ever really loved you, whether I ever truly cared to discover who you really were. (343)

Mariana realizes "that for what is really true there are no words;" thus, her writing allows her to (re)create her self and to escape conformity to a set meaning of the feminine. The absolute truth about an essential femininity which patriarchal discourse encourages her (us) to believe are challenged and the challenge becomes politics and source of pleasure:

> The truth demands that I confess that I for my part found in you only the attraction of rebellion and gay abandon. . . .You were adventure, novelty. . . .It was as though in our love affair I had been the cavalier. . .everything that everyone expected of each of us became completely reversed. (343)

A mere reversal of gender roles would not solve the political problem, but here reversal constitutes one among other resisting strategies of self-representation: Mariana's identity cannot be finally defined as "male," as it could not be defined as despondent, or as deceitful. Like the text's self-reflexivity and the authors' anonymity, Mariana's reversal of gender roles ensures instability of meaning and thus contributes to the process of resistance to fascism.

* * *

As this analysis demonstrates, the three women writers in *New Portuguese Letters* successfully attempt political intervention by exploring several elements of postmodern philosophy. As they establish their work as oppositional, they also problematize and question its oppositional stance. Their textual practice as such rests on the analysis of traditional "truths" about literature, about women, and about political and patriarchal oppression. The "truth," historically disseminated by a phallocentric literary tradition, are questioned through the dramatization of many different voices, the conflagration of different genres, and the work's intertextuality. Ultimately, they are denounced as ideological constructs instrumental in perpetuating oppression.

The plural representations of the seventeenth-century nun are the central metaphor for the kind of political intervention and resistance suggested by this textual practice. The refusal to represent Mariana in any single way is a metaphor for the postmodern proposal of a politics of the uncertain. The book destabilizes the traditional readings of the nun as a passive, heartbroken lover, uncovers the discourses that determine them, but resists the temptation to offer the kind of political intervention that fosters closure. The key, as suggested by this practice, is to maintain the dialogue. Thus, *New Portuguese Letters* is a text where a postmodern stance is coupled with a political agenda and demonstrates the possibility of a politically engaged feminism that shuns essentialisms.

WORKS CITED

Barreno, Maria Isabel, Maria Teresa Horta, and Maria Velho DaCosta. *New Portuguese Letters*. Trans. Helen R. Lane. New York: Doubleday, 1975.

Creed, Barbara. "From Here to Modernity: Feminism and Postmodernism." *A Postmodern Reader*. Ed. Joseph Natoli and Linda Hutcheon. Albany: State University of New York Press, 1993, 398-418.

Day, Robert Adams. *Told in Letters: Epistolary Fiction Before Richardson*. Ann Arbor: University of Michigan Press, 1966.

Diamond, Irene and Lee Quinby, eds. *Feminism and Foucault: Reflections on Resistance*. Boston: Northeastern University Press, 1988.

Felski, Rita. *Beyond Feminist Aesthetics*. Cambridge, MA: Harvard University Press, 1989.

Genette, Gérard. *Introduction à l'architexte*. Paris: Seuil, 1979.

Guilleragues, Gabriel de Lavergne, vicomte de. *The Portuguese Letters*. Trans. Donald E. Ericson. *The Three Marias: New Portuguese Letters*. Ed. Maria Isabel Barreno, Maria Teresa Horta, and Maria Velho da Costa. Trans Helen R. Lane. New York: Doubleday, 1975, 403-429.

Hekman, Susan. *Gender and Knowledge: Elements of a Postmodern Feminism*. Boston: Northeastern University Press, 1990.

Jameson, Fredric. "Postmodernism, Or, The Cultural Logic of Late Capitalism," *New Left Review* 146 (July-August 1984), 53-92.

Jones, Ann Rosalind. "Inscribing Femininity: French Theories of the Feminine." *Making a Difference: Feminist Literary Criticism*. Ed. Gayle Greene and Coppelia Kahn. New York: Methuen, 1985.

Jost, François. "L'Evolution d'un Genre: Le Roman epistolaire dans les lettres occidentales." *Essais de littérature comparée*. Fribourg, Switz.: Editions universitaires, 1968, 380-402.

Kamuf, Peggy. *Fictions of Feminine Desire*. Lincoln: University of Nebraska Press, 1982.

Kauffman, Linda. *Discourses of Desire*. Ithaca: Cornell University Press, 1986.

Landy-Houillon, Isabelle. Introduction. *Lettres Portugaises, Lettres d'une Peruvienne et Autres Romans d'Amour par Lettres*. Ed. Bernard Bray et Isabelle Landy-Houillon. Paris: Flammarion, 1983.

Lane, Helen R. Translator's Preface. *The Three Marias: New Portuguese Letters*, by Maria Isabel Barreno, Maria Teresa Horta, and Maria Velho da Costa. New York: Doubleday, 1975, 7-13.

MacArthur, Elizabeth J. *Extravagant Narratives*. Princeton, New Jersey: Princeton University Press, 1988.

Miller, Nancy K. *Subject to Change: Reading Feminist Writing*. New York: Columbia University Press, 1988.

Morgan, Robin. "International Feminism: A Call for Support of the Three Marias." *Going Too Far*. New York: Random House, 1975, 220-227.

Morris, Meaghan. "The Pirate's Fiancée: Feminist Philosophers, or maybe tonight it will happen." *Feminism and Foucalult: Reflections on Resistance*. Ed. Irene Diamond and Lee Quinby. Boston: Northeastern University Press, 1988, 21-42.

Mourão, Manuela. *Nuns' Stories, Nuns' Voices: Resistance at the Margins of Patriarchal Ideology*. (Manuscript in progress.)

Nicholson, Linda, ed., *Feminism/Postmodernism*. New York: Routledge, 1990.

Spender, Dale. *Mothers of the Novel*. New York: Pandora Press, 1986.

Wittig, Monique and Evelyne Le Garrec, trans. Introduction. *Nouvelles Lettres Portugaises*. Paris: Editions du Seuil, 1973.

STUDIES IN RELIGION AND SOCIETY

1. Anson D. Shupe, **Six Perspectives on New Religions: A Case Study Approach**

2. Barry Cooper, **Michel Foucault: An Introduction to the Study of His Thought**

3. Eileen Barker (ed.), **New Religious Movements: A Perspective for Understanding Society**

4. Christine Elizabeth King, **The Nazi State and the New Religions: Five Case Studies in Non-conformity**

5. David G. Bromley and James T. Richardson (ed.), **The Brainwashing/ Deprogramming Controversy: Sociological, Psychological, Legal and Historical Perspectives**

6. Tom Craig Darrand and Anson Shupe, **Metaphors of Social Control in a Pentecostal Sect**

7. Judith Mary Weightman, **Making Sense of the Jonestown Suicides: A Sociological History of the Peoples Temple**

8. Barbara Hargrove (ed.), **Religion and the Sociology of Knowledge: Modernization and Pluralism in Christian Thought and Structure**

9. Niklas Luhmann, **Religious Dogmatics and the Evolution of Societies**, introduction by Peter Beyer (trans.)

10. Herbert Richardson (ed.), **Constitutional Issues in the Case of Reverend Moon:** *Amicus* **Briefs Presented to the United States Supreme Court**

11. Annette P. Hampshire, **Mormonism in Conflict: The Nauvoo Years**

12. Patricia Werhane and Kendall D'Andrade (ed.), **Profit and Responsibility: Issues in Business and Professional Ethics**

13. James H. Grace, **Sex and Marriage in the Unification Movement: A Sociological Study**

14. Rebecca Moore, **A Sympathetic History of Jonestown: The Moore Family Involvement in Peoples Temple**

15. Tommy H. Poling and J. Frank Kenney, **The Hare Krishna Character Type: A Study of the Sensate Personality**

16. Edward C. Lehman, Jr., **Women Clergy in England: Sexism, Modern Consciousness, and Church Viability**

17. Joseph H. Fichter, **Autobiographies of Conversion**

18. George B. Pepper, **The Boston Heresy Case in View of the Secularization of Religion: A Case Study in the Sociology of Religion**

19. Leo Driedger, **Mennonite Identity in Conflict**

20. Helen Ralston, **Christian Ashrams: A New Religious Movement in Contemporary India**

21. Martha F. Lee, **The Nation of Islam, An American Millenarian Movement**

22. James T. Richardson (ed.), **Money and Power in the New Religions**

23. Sharon Linzey Georgianna, **The Moral Majority and Fundamentalism: Plausibility and Dissonance**

24. Roger O'Toole, (ed.) **Sociological Studies in Roman Catholicism: Historical and Contemporary Perspectives**

25. Frank D. Schubert, **A Sociological Study of Secularization Trends in the American Catholic University: Decatholicizing the Catholic Religious Curriculum**

26. Hal W. French, **A Study of Religious Fanaticism and Responses To It: Adversary Identity**

27. A. D. Wright, **Catholicism and Spanish Society Under the Reign of Philip II, 1555-1598, and Philip III, 1598-1621**

28. Theodore Weinberger, **Strategies for Sustaining Religious Commitment: The Art of the Religious Life**

29. George W. Buchanan, **Biblical and Theological Insights from Ancient and Modern Civil Law**

30. James Thrower, **Marxism-Leninism as the Civil Religion of Soviet Society: God's Commissar**

31. Phebe Davidson (editor), **New Readings of Spiritual Narrative from the Fifteenth to the Twentieth Century: Secular Force and Self-Disclosure**